The Poetry Of Andrew Marvell

Andrew Marvell was born in Winestead-in-Holderness, East Riding of Yorkshire, near Kingston upon Hull on March 31st, 1621.

He was educated at Hull Grammar School and at the age of 13, he attended Trinity College, Cambridge and eventually received his BA degree.

It is thought that in 1642 Marvell travelled in Europe and, while England was embroiled in its civil war, remained there until 1647. During this time his great friend and even greater poet, John Milton, stated that Marvell had mastered four languages, including French, Italian and Spanish.

Marvell's first poems, in Latin and Greek and published whilst still at Cambridge, lamented a visitation of the plague and celebrated the birth of a child to King Charles I and Queen Henrietta Maria. He only belatedly became sympathetic to the successive regimes during the Interregnum after Charles I's execution, which took place on 30 January 1649. His "Horatian Ode", from early 1650, responds with lament to the regicide even as it praises Oliver Cromwell's return from Ireland.

During 1650–52, Marvell served as tutor to the daughter of the Lord General Thomas Fairfax, who had relinquished command of the Parliamentary army to Cromwell. He lived during that time at Nun Appleton Hall, near York, where he continued to write poetry. Probably the best-known poem he wrote at this time is "To His Coy Mistress".

During the period leading to the First Anglo-Dutch War of 1653, Marvell wrote the satirical "Character of Holland" joining in the abuse of the Dutch as "drunken and profane": "This indigested vomit of the Sea, Fell to the Dutch by Just Propriety".

He became a tutor to Cromwell's ward, William Dutton, in 1653 whilst living at Eton. Marvell also wrote several poems in praise of Cromwell, who was by now Lord Protector of England. In 1656 Marvell and Dutton travelled to France, to visit the Protestant Academy of Saumur.

In 1657, Marvell joined Milton, who by that time had lost his sight, in service as Latin secretary to Cromwell's Council of State at a salary of £200 a year. Oliver Cromwell died in 1658 and succeeded as Lord Protector by his son Richard.

In 1659 Marvell was elected Member of Parliament for Kingston-upon-Hull in the Third Protectorate Parliament and re-elected MP for Hull in 1660 for the Convention Parliament. The monarchy was restored to Charles II in 1660. Marvell managed to avoid punishment for his co-operation with republicanism, and he helped convince Charles II not to execute John Milton for his anti-monarchical writings and revolutionary activities.

In 1661 Marvell was re-elected MP for Hull in the Cavalier Parliament. He eventually came to write several long and bitterly satirical verses against the corruption of the court. Although circulated in manuscript form, some finding anonymous publication in print, they were too politically sensitive and thus dangerous to be published under his name until well after his death. Marvell took up opposition to the 'court party', and satirised them anonymously. In his longest verse satire, Last Instructions to a Painter, written in 1667, Marvell responded to the political corruption that had contributed to English failures during the Second Anglo-Dutch War.

From 1659 until his death in 1678, Marvell was serving as London agent for the Hull Trinity House, a shipmasters' guild. He travelled on their behalf to the Dutch Republic and Russia, Sweden, and Denmark.

He died suddenly on August 16th, 1678, while in attendance at a popular meeting of his old constituents at Hull. His health had been remarkably good; and it was speculated that he was poisoned by political or clerical enemies.

Marvell was buried in the church of St Giles in the Fields in central London. His monument, erected by his grateful constituency, bears the following inscription:

Near this place lyeth the body of Andrew Marvell, Esq., a man so endowed by Nature, so improved by Education, Study, and Travel, so consummated by Experience, that, joining the peculiar graces of Wit and Learning, with a singular penetration and strength of judgment; and exercising all these in the whole course of his life, with an unutterable steadiness in the ways of Virtue, he became the ornament and example of his age, beloved by good men, feared by bad, admired by all, though imitated by few; and scarce paralleled by any. But a Tombstone can neither contain his character, nor is Marble necessary to transmit it to posterity; it is engraved in the minds of this generation, and will be always legible in his inimitable writings, nevertheless. He having served twenty years successfully in Parliament, and that with such Wisdom, Dexterity, and Courage, as becomes a true Patriot, the town of Kingston-upon-Hull, from whence he was deputed to that Assembly, lamenting in his death the public loss, have erected this Monument of their Grief and their Gratitude, 1688.

Index Of Poems

To His Coy Mistress

Had we but World enough, and Time,
This coyness Lady were no crime.
We would sit down, and think which way
To walk, and pass our long Loves Day.
Thou by the Indian Ganges side.
Should'st Rubies find: I by the Tide
Of Humber would complain. I would
Love you ten years before the Flood:
And you should if you please refuse
Till the Conversion of the Jews.
My vegetable Love should grow
Vaster then Empires, and more slow.
An hundred years should go to praise
Thine Eyes, and on thy Forehead Gaze.
Two hundred to adore each Breast.
But thirty thousand to the rest.
An Age at least to every part,
And the last Age should show your Heart.
For Lady you deserve this State;
Nor would I love at lower rate.
But at my back I alwaies hear
Times winged Charriot hurrying near:
And yonder all before us lye
Desarts of vast Eternity.
Thy Beauty shall no more be found;
Nor, in thy marble Vault, shall sound

My ecchoing Song: then Worms shall try
That long preserv'd Virginity:
And your quaint Honour turn to durst;
And into ashes all my Lust.
The Grave's a fine and private place,
But none I think do there embrace.
Now therefore, while the youthful hew
Sits on thy skin like morning glew,
And while thy willing Soul transpires
At every pore with instant Fires,
Now let us sport us while we may;
And now, like am'rous birds of prey,
Rather at once our Time devour,
Than languish in his slow-chapt pow'r.
Let us roll all our Strength, and all
Our sweetness, up into one Ball:
And tear our Pleasures with rough strife,
Thorough the Iron gates of Life.
Thus, though we cannot make our Sun
Stand still, yet we will make him run.

A Dialogue Between The Soul And The Body
Soul
O Who shall, from this Dungeon, raise
A Soul inslav'd so many wayes?
With bolts of Bones, that fetter'd stands
In Feet ; and manacled in Hands.
Here blinded with an Eye ; and there
Deaf with the drumming of an Ear.
A Soul hung up, as 'twere, in Chains
Of Nerves, and Arteries, and Veins.
Tortur'd, besides each other part,
In a vain Head, and double Heart.

Body
O who shall me deliver whole,
From bonds of this Tyrannic Soul?
Which, stretcht upright, impales me so,
That mine own Precipice I go;
And warms and moves this needless Frame:
(A Fever could but do the same.)
And, wanting where its spight to try,
Has made me live to let me dye.
A Body that could never rest,
Since this ill Spirit it possest.

Soul
What Magic could me thus confine
Within anothers Grief to pine?

Where whatsoever it complain,
I feel, that cannot feel, the pain.
And all my Care its self employes,
That to preserve, which me destroys:
Constrain'd not only to indure
Diseases, but, whats worse, the Cure:
And ready oft the Port to gain,
Am Shipwrackt into Health again.

Body
But Physick yet could never reach
The Maladies Thou me dost teach;
Whom first the Cramp of Hope does Tear:
And then the Palsie Shakes of Fear.
The Pestilence of Love does heat :
Or Hatred's hidden Ulcer eat.
Joy's chearful Madness does perplex:
Or Sorrow's other Madness vex.
Which Knowledge forces me to know;
And Memory will not foregoe.
What but a Soul could have the wit
To build me up for Sin so fit?
So Architects do square and hew,
Green Trees that in the Forest grew.

A Dialogue, Between the Resolved Soul, And Created Pleasure
Courage my Soul, now learn to wield
The weight of thine immortal Shield.
Close on thy Head thy Helmet bright.
Ballance thy Sword against the Fight.
See where an Army, strong as fair,
With silken Banners spreads the air.
Now, if thou bee'st that thing Divine,
In this day's Combat let it shine:
And shew that Nature wants an Art
To conquer one resolved Heart.

Pleasure
Welcome the Creations Guest,
Lord of Earth, and Heavens Heir.
Lay aside that Warlike Crest,
And of Nature's banquet share:
Where the Souls of fruits and flow'rs
Stand prepar'd to heighten yours.

Soul
I sup above, and cannot stay
To bait so long upon the way.

Pleasure
On these downy Pillows lye,
Whose soft Plumes will thither fly:
On these Roses strow'd so plain
Lest one Leaf thy Side should strain.

Soul
My gentler Rest is on a Thought,
Conscious of doing what I ought.

Pleasure
If thou bee'st with Perfumes pleas'd,
Such as oft the Gods appeas'd,
Thou in fragrant Clouds shalt show
Like another God below.

Soul
A Soul that knowes not to presume
Is Heaven's and its own perfume.

Pleasure
Every thing does seem to vie
Which should first attract thine Eye:
But since none deserves that grace,
In this Crystal view thy face.

Soul
When the Creator's skill is priz'd,
The rest is all but Earth disguis'd.

Pleasure
Heark how Musick then prepares
For thy Stay these charming Aires;
Which the posting Winds recall,
And suspend the Rivers Fall.

Soul
Had I but any time to lose,
On this I would it all dispose.
Cease Tempter. None can chain a mind
Whom this sweet Chordage cannot bind.

Chorus
Earth cannot shew so brave a Sight
As when a single Soul does fence
The Batteries of alluring Sense,
And Heaven views it with delight.
Then persevere: for still new Charges sound:
And if thou overcom'st thou shalt be crown'd.

Pleasure

All this fair, and cost, and sweet,
Which scatteringly doth shine,
Shall within one Beauty meet,
And she be only thine.

Soul
If things of Sight such Heavens be,
What Heavens are those we cannot see?

Pleasure
Where so e're thy Foot shall go
The minted Gold shall lie;
Till thou purchase all below,
And want new Worlds to buy.

Soul
Wer't not a price who 'ld value Gold?
And that's worth nought that can be sold.

Pleasure
Wilt thou all the Glory have
That War or Peace commend?
Half the World shall be thy Slave
The other half thy Friend.

Soul
What Friends, if to my self untrue?
What Slaves, unless I captive you?

Pleasure
Thou shalt know each hidden Cause;
And see the future Time:
Try what depth the Centre draws;
And then to Heaven climb.

Soul
None thither mounts by the degree
Of Knowledge, but Humility.

Chorus
Triumph, triumph, victorious Soul;
The World has not one Pleasure more:
The rest does lie beyond the pole,
And is thine everlasting Store.

A Garden, Written After The Civil Wars
See how the flowers, as at parade,
Under their colours stand display'd:
Each regiment in order grows,

That of the tulip, pink, and rose.
But when the vigilant patrol
Of stars walks round about the pole,
Their leaves, that to the stalks are curl'd,
Seem to their staves the ensigns furl'd.
Then in some flower's beloved hut
Each bee, as sentinel, is shut,
And sleeps so too; but if once stirr'd,
She runs you through, nor asks the word.
O thou, that dear and happy Isle,
The garden of the world erewhile,
Thou Paradise of the four seas
Which Heaven planted us to please,
But, to exclude the world, did guard
With wat'ry if not flaming sword;
What luckless apple did we taste
To make us mortal and thee waste!
Unhappy! shall we never more
That sweet militia restore,
When gardens only had their towers,
And all the garrisons were flowers;
When roses only arms might bear,
And men did rosy garlands wear?

An Epitaph
Enough; and leave the rest to Fame!
'Tis to commend her, but to name.
Courtship which, living, she declined,
When dead, to offer were unkind:
Nor can the truest wit, or friend,
Without detracting, her commend.

To say, she lived a virgin chaste
In this age loose and all unlaced;
Nor was, when vice is so allowed,
Of virtue or ashamed or proud;
That her soul was on Heaven so bent,
No minute but it came and went;
That, ready her last debt to pay,
She summ'd her life up every day;
Modest as morn, as mid-day bright,
Gentle as evening, cool as night:
'Tis true; but all too weakly said.
'Twas more significant, she's dead.

The First Anniversary Of The Government Under Oliver Cromwell
Like the vain Curlings of the Watry maze,

Which in smooth streams a sinking Weight does raise;
So Man, declining alwayes, disappears.
In the Weak Circles of increasing Years;
And his short Tumults of themselves Compose,
While flowing Time above his Head does close.
Cromwell alone with greater Vigour runs,
(Sun-like) the Stages of succeeding Suns:
And still the Day which he doth next restore,
Is the just Wonder of the Day before.
Cromwell alone doth with new Lustre spring,
And shines the Jewel of the yearly Ring.
'Tis he the force of scatter'd Time contracts,
And in one Year the Work of Ages acts:
While heavy Monarchs make a wide Return,
Longer, and more Malignant then Saturn:
And though they all Platonique years should raign,
In the same Posture would be found again.
Their earthly Projects under ground they lay,
More slow and brittle then the China clay:
Well may they strive to leave them to their Son,
For one Thing never was by one King don.
Yet some more active for a Frontier Town
Took in by Proxie, beggs a false Renown;
Another triumphs at the publick Cost,
And will have Wonn, if he no more have Lost;
They fight by Others, but in Person wrong,
And only are against their Subjects strong;
Their other Wars seem but a feign'd contest,
This Common Enemy is still opprest;
If Conquerors, on them they turn their might;
If Conquered, on them they wreak their Spight:
They neither build the Temple in their dayes,
Nor Matter for succeeding Founders raise;
Nor Sacred Prophecies consult within,
Much less themselves to perfect them begin,
No other care they bear of things above,
But with Astrologers divine, and Jove,
To know how long their Planet yet Reprives
From the deserved Fate their guilty lives:
Thus (Image-like) and useless time they tell,
And with vain Scepter strike the hourly Bell;
Nor more contribute to the state of Things,
Then wooden Heads unto the Viols strings,
While indefatigable Cromwell hyes,
And cuts his way still nearer to the Skyes,
Learning a Musique in the Region clear,
To tune this lower to that higher Sphere.
So when Amphion did the Lute command,
Which the God gave him, with his gentle hand,
The rougher Stones, unto his Measures hew'd,
Dans'd up in order from the Quarreys rude;

This took a Lower, that an Higher place,
As he the Treble alter'd, or the Base:
No Note he struck, but a new Story lay'd,
And the great Work ascended while he play'd.
The listning Structures he with Wonder ey'd,
And still new Stopps to various Time apply'd:
Now through the Strings a Martial rage he throws,
And joyng streight the Theban Tow'r arose;
Then as he strokes them with a Touch more sweet,
The flocking Marbles in a Palace meet;
But, for he most the graver Notes did try,
Therefore the Temples rear'd their Columns high:
Thus, ere he ceas'd, his sacred Lute creates
Th'harmonious City of the seven Gates.
Such was that wondrous Order and Consent,
When Cromwell tun'd the ruling Instrument;
While tedious Statesmen many years did hack,
Framing a Liberty that still went back;
Whose num'rous Gorge could swallow in an hour
That Island, which the Sea cannot devour:
Then our Amphion issues out and sings,
And once he struck, and twice, the pow'rful Strings.
The Commonwealth then first together came,
And each one enter'd in the willing Frame;
All other Matter yields, and may be rul'd;
But who the Minds of stubborn Men can build?
No Quarry bears a Stone so hardly wrought,
Nor with such labour from its Center brought;
None to be sunk in the Foundation bends,
Each in the House the highest Place contends,
And each the Hand that lays him will direct,
And some fall back upon the Architect;
Yet all compos'd by his attractive Song,
Into the Animated City throng.
The Common-wealth does through their Centers all
Draw the Circumf'rence of the publique Wall;
The crossest Spirits here do take their part,
Fast'ning the Contignation which they thwart;
And they, whose Nature leads them to divide,
Uphold, this one, and that the other Side;
But the most Equal still sustein the Height,
And they as Pillars keep the Work upright;
While the resistance of opposed Minds,
The Fabrick as with Arches stronger binds,
Which on the Basis of a Senate free,
Knit by the Roofs Protecting weight agree.
When for his foot he thus a place had found,
He hurles e'r since the World about him round,
And in his sev'ral Aspects, like a Star,
Here shines in Peace, and thither shoots a War.
While by his Beams observing Princes steer,

And wisely court the Influence they fear,
O would they rather by his Pattern won.
Kiss the approaching, nor yet angry Son;
And in their numbred Footsteps humbly tread
The path where holy Oracles do lead;
How might they under such a Captain raise
The great Designs kept for the latter Dayes!
But mad with reason, so miscall'd, of State
They know them not, and what they know not, hate
Hence still they sing Hosanna to the Whore,
And her whom they should Massacre adore:
But Indians whom they should convert, subdue;
Nor teach, but traffique with, or burn the Jew.
Unhappy Princes, ignorantly bred,
By Malice some, by Errour more misled;
If gracious Heaven to my Life give length,
Leisure to Times, and to my Weakness Strength,
Then shall I once with graver Accents shake
Your Regal sloth, and your long Slumbers wake:
Like the shrill Huntsman that prevents the East,
Winding his Horn to Kings that chase the Beast.
Till then my Muse shall hollow far behind
Angelique Cromwell who outwings the wind;
And in dark Nights, and in cold Dayes alone
Pursues the Monster thorough every Throne:
Which shrinking to her Roman Den impure,
Gnashes her Goary teeth; nor there secure.
Hence oft I think, if in some happy Hour
High Grace should meet in one with highest Pow'r,
And then a seasonable People still
Should bend to his, as he to Heavens will,
What we might hope, what wonderful Effect
From such a wish'd Conjuncture might reflect.
Sure, the mysterious Work, where none withstand,
Would forthwith finish under such a Hand:
Fore-shortned Time its useless Course would stay,
And soon precipitate the latest Day.
But a thick Cloud about that Morning lyes,
And intercepts the Beams of Mortal eyes,
That 'tis the most which we deteremine can,
If these the Times, then this must be the Man.
And well he therefore does, and well has guest,
Who in his Age has always forward prest:
And knowing not where Heavens choice may light,
Girds yet his Sword, and ready stands to fight;
But Men alas, as if they nothing car'd,
Look on, all unconcern'd, or unprepar'd;
And Stars still fall, and still the Dragons Tail
Swinges the Volumes of its horrid Flail.
For the great Justice that did first suspend
The World by Sin, does by the same extend.

Hence that blest Day still counterpoysed wastes,
The ill delaying, what th' Elected hastes;
Hence landing Nature to new Seas it tost,
And good Designes still with their Authors lost.
And thou, great Cromwell, for whose happy birth
A Mold was chosen out of better Earth;
Whose Saint-like Mother we did lately see
Live out an Age, long as a Pedigree;
That she might seem, could we the Fall dispute,
T'have smelt the Blossome, and not eat the Fruit;
Though none does of more lasting Parents grow,
But never any did them Honor so;
Though thou thine Heart from Evil still unstain'd,
And always hast thy Tongue from fraud refrain'd,
Thou, who so oft through Storms of thundring Lead
Hast born securely thine undaunted Head,
Thy Brest through ponyarding Conspiracies,
Drawn from the Sheath of lying Prophecies;
Thee proof beyond all other Force or Skill,
Our Sins endanger, and shall one day kill.
How near they fail'd, and in thy sudden Fall
At once assay'd to overturn us all.
Our brutish fury strugling to be Free,
Hurry'd thy Horses while they hurry'd thee.
When thou hadst almost quit thy Mortal cares,
And soyl'd in Dust thy Crown of silver Hairs.
Let this one Sorrow interweave among
The other Glories of our yearly Song.
Like skilful Looms which through the costly threed
Of purling Ore, a shining wave do shed:
So shall the Tears we on past Grief employ,
Still as they trickle, glitter in our Joy.
So with more Modesty we may be True,
And speak as of the Dead the Praises due:
While impious Men deceiv'd with pleasure short,
On their own Hopes shall find the Fall retort.
But the poor Beasts wanting their noble Guide,
What could they move? shrunk guiltily aside.
First winged Fear transports them far away,
And leaden Sorrow then their flight did stay.
See how they each his towring Crest abate,
And the green Grass, and their known Mangers hate,
Nor through wide Nostrils snuffe the wanton air,
Nor their round Hoofs, or curled Mane'scompare;
With wandring Eyes, and restless Ears theystood,
And with shrill Neighings ask'd him of the Wood.
Thou Cromwell falling, not a stupid Tree,
Or Rock so savage, but it mourn'd for thee:
And all about was heard a Panique groan,
As if that Natures self were overthrown.
It seem'd the Earth did from the Center tear;

It seem'd the Sun was faln out of the Sphere:
Justice obstructed lay, and Reason fool'd;
Courage disheartned, and Religion cool'd.
A dismal Silence through the Palace went,
And then loud Shreeks the vaulted Marbles rent.
Such as the dying Chorus sings by turns,
And to deaf Seas, and ruthless Tempests mourns,
When now they sink, and now the plundring Streams
Break up each Deck, and rip the Oaken seams.
But thee triumphant hence the firy Carr,
And firy Steeds had born out of the Warr,
From the low World, and thankless Men above,
Unto the Kingdom blest of Peace and Love:
We only mourn'd our selves, in thine Ascent,
Whom thou hadst lest beneath with Mantle rent.
For all delight of Life thou then didst lose,
When to Command, thou didst thy self Depose;
Resigning up thy Privacy so dear,
To turn the headstrong Peoples Charioteer;
For to be Cromwell was a greater thing,
Then ought below, or yet above a King:
Therefore thou rather didst thy Self depress,
Yielding to Rule, because it made thee Less.
For, neither didst thou from the first apply
Thy sober Spirit unto things too High,
But in thine own Fields exercisedst long,
An Healthful Mind within a Body strong;
Till at the Seventh time thou in the Skyes,
As a small Cloud, like a Mans hand didst rise;
Then did thick Mists and Winds the air deform,
And down at last thou pow'rdst the fertile Storm;
Which to the thirsty Land did plenty bring,
But though forewarn'd, o'r-took and wet the King.
What since he did, an higher Force him push'd
Still from behind, and it before him rush'd,
Though undiscern'd among the tumult blind,
Who think those high Decrees by Man design'd.
'Twas Heav'n would not that his Pow'r should cease,
But walk still middle betwixt War and Peace;
Choosing each Stone, and poysing every weight,
Trying the Measures of the Bredth and Height;
Here pulling down, and there erecting New,
Founding a firm State by Proportions true.
When Gideon so did from the War retreat,
Yet by Conquest of two Kings grown great,
He on the Peace extends a Warlike power,
And Is'rel silent saw him rase the Tow'r;
And how he Succoths Elders durst suppress,
With Thorns and Briars of the Wilderness.
No King might ever such a Force have done;
Yet would not he be Lord, nor yet his Son.

Thou with the same strength, and an Heart as plain,
Didst (like thine Olive) still refuse to Reign;
Though why should others all thy Labor spoil,
And Brambles be anointed with thine Oyl,
Whose climbing Flame, without a timely stop,
Had quickly Levell'd every Cedar's top.
Therefore first growing to thy self a Law,
Th'ambitious Shrubs thou in just time didst aw.
So have I seen at Sea, when whirling Winds,
Hurry the Bark, but more the Seamens minds,
Who with mistaken Course salute the Sand,
And threat'ning Rocks misapprehend for Land;
While baleful Tritons to the shipwrack guide.
And Corposants along the Tacklings slide.
The Passengers all wearyed out before,
Giddy, and wishing for the fatal Shore;
Some lusty Mate, who with more careful Eye
Counted the Hours, and ev'ry Star did spy,
The Helm does from the artless Steersman strain,
And doubles back unto the safer Main.
What though a while they grumble discontent,
Saving himself he does their loss prevent.
'Tis not a Freedome, that where All command;
Nor Tyranny, where One does them withstand:
But who of both the Bounders knows to lay
Him as their Father must the State obey.
Thou, and thine House, like Noah's Eight did rest,
Left by the Wars Flood on the Mountains crest:
And the large Vale lay subject to thy Will,
Which thou but as an Husbandman would Till:
And only didst for others plant the Vine
Of Liberty, not drunken with its Wine.
That sober Liberty which men may have,
That they enjoy, but more they vainly crave:
And such as to their Parents Tents do press,
May shew their own, not see his Nakedness.
Yet such a Chammish issue still does rage,
The Shame and Plague both of the Land and Age,
Who watch'd thy halting, and thy Fall deride,
Rejoycing when thy Foot had slipt aside;
that their new King might the fifth Scepter shake,
And make the World, by his Example, Quake:
Whose frantique Army should they want for Men
Might muster Heresies, so one were ten.
What thy Misfortune, they the Spirit call,
And their Religion only is to Fall.
Oh Mahomet! now couldst thou rise again,
Thy Falling-sickness should have made thee Reign,
While Feake and Simpson would in many a Tome,
Have writ the Comments of thy sacred Foame:
For soon thou mightst have past among their Rant

Wer't but for thine unmoved Tulipant;
As thou must needs have own'd them of thy band
For prophecies fit to be Alcorand.
Accursed Locusts, whom your King does spit
Out of the Center of th'unbottom'd Pit;
Wand'rers, Adult'rers, Lyers, Munser's rest,
Sorcerers, Atheists, Jesuites, Possest;
You who the Scriptures and the Laws deface
With the same liberty as Points and Lace;
Oh Race most hypocritically strict!
Bent to reduce us to the ancient Pict;
Well may you act the Adam and the Eve;
Ay, and the Serpent too that did deceive.
But the great Captain, now the danger's ore,
Makes you for his sake Tremble one fit more;
And, to your spight, returning yet alive
Does with himself all that is good revive.
So when first Man did through the Morning new
See the bright Sun his shining Race pursue,
All day he follow'd with unwearied sight,
Pleas'd with that other World of moving Light;
But thought him when he miss'd his setting beams,
Sunk in the Hills, or plung'd below the Streams.
While dismal blacks hung round the Universe,
And Stars (like Tapers) burn'd upon his Herse:
And Owls and Ravens with their screeching noyse
Did make the Fun'rals sadder by their Joyes.
His weeping Eyes the doleful Vigils keep,
Not knowing yet the Night was made for sleep:
Still to the West, where he him lost, he turn'd,
And with such accents, as Despairing, mourn'd:
Why did mine Eyes once see so bright a Ray;
Or why Day last no longer than a Day?
When streight the Sun behind him he descry'd,
Smiling serenely from the further side.
So while our Star that gives us Light and Heat,
Seem'd now a long and gloomy Night to threat,
Up from the other World his Flame he darts,
And Princes shining through their windows starts;
Who their suspected Counsellors refuse,
And credulous Ambassadors accuse.
"Is this, saith one, the Nation that we read
"Spent with both Wars, under a Captain dead?
"Yet rig a Navy while we dress us late;
"And ere we Dine, rase and rebuild our State.
"What Oaken Forrests, and what golden Mines!
"What Mints of Men, what Union of Designes!
"Unless their Ships, do, as their Fowle proceed
"Of shedding Leaves, that with their Ocean breed.
"Theirs are not Ships, but rather Arks of War,
"And beaked Promontories sail'd from far;

"Of floting Islands a new Hatched Nest;
"A Fleet of Worlds, of other Worlds in quest;
"An hideous shole of wood Leviathans,
"Arm'd with three Tire of brazen Hurricans;
"That through the Center shoot their thundring side
"And sink the Earth that does at Anchor ride.
'What refuge to escape them can be found,
"Whose watry Leaguers all the world surround?
"Needs must we all their Tributaries be,
"Whose Navies hold the Sluces of the Sea.
"The Ocean is the Fountain of Command,
"But that once took, we Captives are on Land:
"And those that have the Waters for their share,
"Can quickly leave us neither Earth nor Air.
"Yet if through these our Fears could find a pass;
"Through double Oak, & lin'd with treble Brass;
"That one Man still, although but nam'd, alarms
"More then all Men, all Navies, and all Arms.
"Him, all the Day, Him, in late Nights I dread,
"And still his Sword seems hanging o're my head.
"The Nation had been ours, but his one Soul
"Moves the great Bulk, and animates the whole.
"He Secrecy with Number hath inchas'd,
"Courage with Age, Maturity with Hast:
"The Valiants Terror, Riddle of the Wise;
"And still his Fauchion all our Knots unties.
"Where did he learn those Arts that cost us dear?
"Where below Earth, or where above the Sphere?
"He seems a King by long Succession born,
"And yet the same to be a King does scorn.
"Abroad a King he seems, and something more,
"At Home a Subject on the equal Floor.
"O could I once him with our Title see,
"So should I hope yet he might Dye as wee.
"But let them write his Praise that love him best,
"It grieves me sore to have thus much confest.
"Pardon, great Prince, if thus their Fear or Spight
"More then our Love and Duty do thee Right.
"I yield, nor further will the Prize contend;
"So that we both alike may miss our End:
"While thou thy venerable Head dost raise
"As far above their Malice as my Praise.
"And as the Angel of our Commonweal,
"Troubling the Waters, yearly mak'st them Heal.

An Horatian Ode Upon Cromwell's Return From Ireland
The forward youth that would appear
Must now forsake his muses dear,
Nor in the shadows sing,

His numbers languishing.
'Tis time to leave the books in dust,
And oil the unusèd armour's rust:
Removing from the wall
The corslet of the hall.
So restless Cromwell could not cease
In the inglorious arts of peace,
But through adventurous war
Urgèd his active star.
And, like the three-forked lightning, first
Breaking the clouds where it was nursed,
Did thorough his own side
His fiery way divide.
(For 'tis all one to courage high
The emulous or enemy:
And with such to inclose
Is more than to oppose.)
Then burning through the air he went,
And palaces and temples rent:
And Cæsar's head at last
Did through his laurels blast.
'Tis madness to resist or blame
The force of angry heaven's flame:
And, if we would speak true,
Much to the man is due,
Who from his private gardens, where
He lived reservèd and austere,
As if his highest plot
To plant the bergamot,
Could by industrious valour climb
To ruin the great work of time,
And cast the kingdoms old
Into another mould.
Though justice against fate complain,
And plead the ancient rights in vain:
But those do hold or break
As men are strong or weak.
Nature, that hateth emptiness,
Allows of penetration less:
And therefore must make room
Where greater spirits come.
What field of all the Civil Wars,
Where his were not the deepest scars?
And Hampton shows what part
He had of wiser art,
Where, twining subtle fears with hope,
He wove a net of such a scope,
That Charles himself might chase
To Carisbrooke's narrow case:
That then the royal actor born
The tragic scaffold might adorn:

While round the armèd bands
Did clap their bloody hands.
He nothing common did or mean
Upon that memorable scene:
But with his keener eye
The axe's edge did try:
Nor called the gods with vulgar spite
To vindicate his helpless right,
But bowed his comely head,
Down, as upon a bed.
This was that memorable hour
Which first assured the forcèd power.
So when they did design
The Capitol's first line,
A bleeding head where they begun,
Did fright the architects to run;
And yet in that the State
Foresaw its happy fate.
And now the Irish are ashamed
To see themselves in one year tamed:
So much one man can do,
That does both act and know.
They can affirm his praises best,
And have, though overcome, confessed
How good he is, how just,
And fit for highest trust:
Nor yet grown stiffer with command,
But still in the Republic's hand:
How fit he is to sway
That can so well obey.
He to the Commons feet presents
A kingdom, for his first year's rents:
And, what he may, forbears
His fame, to make it theirs:
And has his sword and spoils ungirt,
To lay them at the public's skirt.
So when the falcon high
Falls heavy from the sky,
She, having killed, no more does search
But on the next green bough to perch,
Where, when he first does lure,
The falc'ner has her sure.
What may not then our isle presume
While Victory his crest does plume?
What may not others fear
If thus he crowns each year?
A Cæ.sar, he, ere long to Gaul,
To Italy an Hannibal,
And to all states not free
Shall climactéric be.
The Pict no shelter now whall find

Within his parti-coloured mind,
But from this valour sad
Shrink underneath the plaid:
Happy, if in the tufted brake
The English hunter him mistake,
Nor lay his hounds in near
The Caledonian deer.
But thou, the Wars' and Fortune's son,
March indefatigably on,
And for the last effect
Still keep thy sword erect:
Besides the force it has to fright
The spirits of the shady night,
The same arts that did gain
A power, must it maintain.

Daphnis And Chloe
Daphnis must from Chloe part:
Now is come the dismal Hour
That must all his Hopes devour,
All his Labour, all his Art.

Nature, her own Sexes foe,
Long had taught her to be coy:
But she neither knew t' enjoy,
Nor yet let her Lover go.

But, with this sad News surpriz'd,
Soon she let that Niceness fall;
And would gladly yield to all,
So it had his stay compriz'd.

Nature so her self does use
To lay by her wonted State,
Left the World should separate;
Sudden Parting closer glews.

He, well read in all the wayes
By which men their Siege maintain,
Knew not that the Fort to gain
Better 'twas the siege to raise.

But he came so full possest
With the Grief of Parting thence,
That he had not so much Sence
As to see he might be blest.

Till Love in her Language breath'd
Words she never spake before;

But then Legacies no more
To a dying Man bequeath'd.

For, Alas, the time was spent,
Now the latest minut's run
When poor Daphnis is undone,
Between Joy and Sorrow rent.

At that Why, that Stay my Dear,
His disorder'd Locks he tare;
And with rouling Eyes did glare,
And his cruel Fate forswear.

As the Soul of one scarce dead,
With the shrieks of Friends aghast,
Looks distracted back in hast,
And then streight again is fled.

So did wretched Daphnis look,
Frighting her he loved most.
At the last, this Lovers Ghost
Thus his Leave resolved took.

Are my Hell and Heaven Joyn'd
More to torture him that dies?
Could departure not suffice,
But that you must then grow kind?

Ah my Chloe how have I
Such a wretched minute found,
When thy Favours should me wound
More than all thy Cruelty?

So to the condemned Wight
The delicious Cup we fill;
And allow him all he will,
For his last and short Delight.

But I will not now begin
Such a Debt unto my Foe;
Nor to my Departure owe
What my Presence could not win.

Absence is too much alone:
Better 'tis to go in peace,
Than my Losses to increase
By a late Fruition.

Why should I enrich my Fate?
'Tis a Vanity to wear,
For my Executioner,

Jewels of so high a rate.

Rather I away will pine
In a manly stubborness
Than be fatted up express
For the Canibal to dine.

Whilst this grief does thee disarm,
All th' Enjoyment of our Love
But the ravishment would prove
Of a Body dead while warm.

And I parting should appear
Like the Gourmand Hebrew dead,
While he Quailes and Manna fed,
And does through the Desert err.

Or the Witch that midnight wakes
For the Fern, whose magick Weed
In one minute casts the Seed.
And invisible him makes.

Gentler times for Love are ment:
Who for parting pleasure strain
Gather Roses in the rain,
Wet themselves and spoil their Sent.

Farewel therefore all the fruit
Which I could from Love receive:
Joy will not with Sorrow weave,
Nor will I this Grief pollute.

Fate I come, as dark, as sad,
As thy Malice could desire;
Yet bring with me all the Fire
That Love in his Torches had.

At these words away he broke;
As who long has praying ly'n,
To his Heads-man makes the Sign,
And receives the parting stroke.

But hence Virgins all beware.
Last night he with Phlogis slept;
This night for Dorinda kept;
And but rid to take the Air.

Yet he does himself excuse;
Nor indeed without a Cause.
For, according to the Lawes,
Why did Chloe once refuse?

The Gallery

Clora come view my Soul, and tell
Whether I have contriv'd it well.
Now all its several lodgings lye
Compos'd into one Gallery;
And the great Arras-hangings, made
Of various Faces, by are laid;
That, for all furniture, you'l find
Only your Picture in my Mind.

Here Thou art painted in the Dress
Of an Inhumane Murtheress;
Examining upon our Hearts
Thy fertile Shop of cruel Arts:
Engines more keen than ever yet
Adorned Tyrants Cabinet;
Of which the most tormenting are
Black Eyes, red Lips, and curled Hair.

But, on the other side, th' art drawn
Like to Aurora in the Dawn;
When in the East she slumb'ring lyes,
And stretches out her milky Thighs;
While all the morning Quire does sing,
And Mamma falls, and Roses spring;
And, at thy Feet, the wooing Doves
Sit perfecting their harmless Loves.

Like an Enchantress here thou show'st,
Vexing thy restless Lover's Ghost;
And, by a Light obscure, dost rave
Over his Entrails, in the Cave;
Divining thence, with horrid Care,
How long thou shalt continue fair;
And (when inform'd) them throw'st away,
To be the greedy Vultur's prey.

But, against that, thou sit'st a float
Like Venus in her pearly Boat.
The Halcyons, calming all that's nigh,
Betwixt the Air and Water fly.
Or, if some rowling Wave appears,
A Mass of Ambergris it bears.
Nor blows more Wind than what may well
Convoy the Perfume to the Smell.

These Pictures and a thousand more,
Of Thee, my Gallery dost store;

In all the Forms thou can'st invent
Either to please me, or torment:
For thou alone to people me,
Art grown a num'rous Colony;
And a Collection choicer far
Then or White-hall's, or Mantua's were.

But, of these Pictures and the rest,
That at the Entrance likes me best:
Where the same Posture, and the Look
Remains, with which I first was took.
A tender Shepherdess, whose Hair
Hangs loosely playing in the Air,
Transplanting Flow'rs from the green Hill,
To crown her Head, and Bosome fill.

The Garden
How vainly men themselves amaze
To win the Palm, the Oke, or Bayes;
And their uncessant Labours see
Crown'd from some single Herb or Tree,
Whose short and narrow verged Shade
Does prudently their Toyles upbraid;
While all Flow'rs and all Trees do close
To weave the Garlands of repose.

Fair quiet, have I found thee here,
And Innocence thy Sister dear!
Mistaken long, I sought you then
In busie Companies of Men.
Your sacred Plants, if here below,
Only among the Plants will grow.
Society is all but rude,
To this delicious Solitude.

No white nor red was ever seen
So am'rous as this lovely green.
Fond Lovers, cruel as their Flame,
Cut in these Trees their Mistress name.
Little, Alas, they know, or heed,
How far these Beauties Hers exceed!
Fair Trees! where s'eer you barkes I wound,
No Name shall but your own be found.

When we have run our Passions heat,
Love hither makes his best retreat.
The Gods, that mortal Beauty chase,
The Gods, that mortal Beauty chase,
Apollo hunted Daphne so,

Only that She might Laurel grow.
And Pan did after Syrinx speed,
Not as a Nymph, but for a Reed.

What wond'rous Life in this I lead!
Ripe Apples drop about my head;
The Luscious Clusters of the Vine
Upon my Mouth do crush their Wine;
The Nectaren, and curious Peach,
Into my hands themselves do reach;
Stumbling on Melons, as I pass,
Insnar'd with Flow'rs, I fall on Grass.

Mean while the Mind, from pleasure less,
Withdraws into its happiness:
The Mind, that Ocean where each kind
Does streight its own resemblance find;
Yet it creates, transcending these,
Far other Worlds, and other Seas;
Annihilating all that's made
To a green Thought in a green Shade.

Here at the Fountains sliding foot,
Or at some Fruit-tress mossy root,
Casting the Bodies Vest aside,
My Soul into the boughs does glide:
There like a Bird it sits, and sings,
Then whets, and combs its silver Wings;
And, till prepar'd for longer flight,
Waves in its Plumes the various Light.

Such was that happy Garden-state,
While Man there walk'd without a Mate:
After a Place so pure, and sweet,
What other Help could yet be meet!
But 'twas beyond a Mortal's share
To wander solitary there:
Two Paradises 'twere in one
To live in Paradise alone.

How well the skilful Gardner drew
Of flow'rs and herbes this Dial new;
Where from above the milder Sun
Does through a fragrant Zodiack run;
And, as it works, th' industrious Bee
Computes its time as well as we.
How could such sweet and wholsome Hours
Be reckon'd but with herbs and flow'rs!

Yet they by restless toil became at length,
So proud and confident of their made strength,
That they with joy their boasting general heard,
Wish then for that assault he lately feared.
His wish he has, for now undaunted Blake,
With wingèd speed, for Santa Cruz does make.
For your renown, his conquering fleet does ride,
O'er seas as vast as is the Spaniards' pride.
Whose fleet and trenches viewed, he soon did say,
`We to their strength are more obliged than they.
Were't not for that, they from their fate would run,
And a third world seek out, our arms to shun.
Those forts, which there so high and strong appear,
Do not so much suppress, as show their fear.
Of speedy victory let no man doubt,
Our worst work's past, now we have found them out.
Behold their navy does at anchor lie,
And they are ours, for now they cannot fly.'

This said, the whole fleet gave it their applause,
And all assumes your courage, in your cause.
That bay they enter, which unto them owes,
The noblest of wreaths, that victory bestows.
Bold Stayner leads: this fleet's designed by fate,
To give him laurel, as the last did plate.

The thundering cannon now begins the fight,
And though it be at noon creates a night.
The air was soon after the fight begun,
Far more enflamed by it than by the sun.
Never so burning was that climate known,
War turned the temperate to the torrid zone.

Fate these two fleets between both worlds had brought,
Who fight, as if for both those worlds they fought.
Thousands of ways thousands of men there die,
Some ships are sunk, some blown up in the sky.
Nature ne'er made cedars so high aspire,
As oaks did then urged by the active fire,
Which by quick powder's force, so high was sent,
That it returned to its own element.
Torn limbs some leagues into the island fly,
Whilst others lower in the sea do lie,
Scarce souls from bodies severed are so far
By death, as bodies there were by the war.
The all-seeing sun, ne'er gazed on such a sight,
Two dreadful navies there at anchor fight.
And neither have or power or will to fly,
There one must conquer, or there both must die.
Far different motives yet engaged them thus,
Necessity did them, but Choice did us.

A choice which did the highest worth express,
And was attended by as high success.
For your resistless genius there did reign,
By which we laurels reaped e'en on the main.
So properous stars, though absent to the sense,
Bless those they shine for, by their influence.

Our cannon now tears every ship and sconce,
And o'er two elements triumphs at once.
Their gallions sunk, their wealth the sea doth fill
The only place where it can cause no ill.

Ah, would those treasures which both Indies have,
Were buried in as large, and deep a grave,
Wars' chief support with them would buried be,
And the land owe her peace unto the sea.
Ages to come your conquering arms will bless,
There they destroy what had destroyed their peace.
And in one war the present age may boast
The certain seeds of many wars are lost.

All the foe's ships destroyed, by sea or fire,
Victorious Blake, does from the bay retire,
His siege of Spain he then again pursues,
And there first brings of his success the news:
The saddest news that e'er to Spain was brought,
Their rich fleet sunk, and ours with laurel fraught,
Whilst fame in every place her trumpet blows,
And tells the world how much to you it owes.

Bermudas
Where the remote Bermudas ride
In th' Oceans bosome unespy'd,
From a small Boat, that row'd along,
The listning Winds receiv'd this Song.
What should we do but sing his Praise
That led us through the watry Maze,
Unto an Isle so long unknown,
And yet far kinder than our own?
Where he the huge Sea-Monsters wracks,
That lift the Deep upon their Backs.
He lands us on a grassy stage;
Safe from the Storms, and Prelat's rage.
He gave us this eternal Spring,
Which here enamells every thing;
And sends the Fowl's to us in care,
On daily Visits through the Air,
He hangs in shades the Orange bright,

Like golden Lamps in a green Night.
And does in the Pomgranates close,
Jewels more rich than Ormus show's.
He makes the Figs our mouths to meet;
And throws the Melons at our feet.
But Apples plants of such a price,
No Tree could ever bear them twice.
With Cedars, chosen by his hand,
From Lebanon, he stores the Land.
And makes the hollow Seas, that roar,
Proclaime the Ambergris on shoar.
He cast (of which we rather boast)
The Gospels Pearl upon our coast.
And in these Rocks for us did frame
A Temple, where to sound his Name.
Oh let our Voice his Praise exalt,
Till it arrive at Heavens Vault:
Which thence (perhaps) rebounding, may
Eccho beyond the Mexique Bay.
Thus sung they, in the English boat,
An holy and a chearful Note,
And all the way, to guide their Chime,
With falling Oars they kept the time.

Nostradamus' Prophecy.
For faults and follies London's doom shall fix,
And she must sink in flames in sixty-six.
Fire-balls shall fly, but few shall see the train,
As far as from Whitehall to Pudding-lane,
To burn the city, which again shall rise,
Beyond all hopes, aspiring to the skies,
Where Vengeance dwells. But there is one thing more
(Tho its walls stand) shall bring the city low'r;
When legislators shall their trust betray.
Saving their own, shall give the rest away;
And those false men, by the easy people sent.
Give taxes to the king by Parliament;
When barefac'd villains shall not blush to cheat,
And Chequer-doors shall shut up Lombard-street;
When players come to act the part of queens,
Within the curtains, and behind the scenes;
When sodomy shall be prime min'ster's sport.
And whoring shall be the least crime at Court;
When boys shall take their sisters for their mate.
And practise incest between seven and eight;
When no man knows in whom to put his trust,
And e'en to rob the Chequer shall be just;
When Declarations, lies, and every oath,
Shall be in use at Court, but faith and troth;

When two good kings shall be at Brentford town,
And when in London there shall not be one;
When the seat's given to a talking fool,
Whom wise men laugh at, and whom women rule,
A min'ster able only in his tongue,
To make harsh empty speeches two hours long;
When an old Scotch Covenanter shall be
The champion for the English hierarchy;
When bishops shall lay all religion by,
And strive by law t' establish tyranny;
When a lean Treasurer shall in one year
Make himself fat, his king and people bare;
When th' English prince shall Englishmen despise,
And think French only loyal, Irish wise;
When wooden shoon shall be the English wear.
And Magna Charta shall no more appear
Then th' English shall a greater tyrant know,
Than either Greek or Latin story show;
Their wives to's lust expos'd, their wealth to's spoil.
With groans, to fill his Treasury, they toil;
But like the Bellides must sigh in vain,
For that still fill'd flows out as fast again;
Then they with envious eyes shall Belgium see,
And wish in vain Venetian liberty.
The frogs too late, grown weary of their pain,
Shall pray to Jove to take him back again.

The Match
Nature had long a Treasure made
Of all her choisest store;
Fearing, when She should be decay'd,
To beg in vain for more.

Her Orientest Colours there,
And Essences most pure,
With sweetest Perfumes hoarded were,
All as she thought secure.

She seldom them unlock'd, or us'd,
But with the nicest care;
For, with one grain of them diffus'd,
She could the World repair.

But likeness soon together drew
What she did separate lay;
Of which one perfect Beauty grew,
And that was Celia.

Love wisely had of long fore-seen

That he must once grow old;
And therefore stor'd a Magazine,
To save him from the cold.

He kept the several Cells repleat
With Nitre thrice refin'd;
The Naphta's and the Sulphurs heat,
And all that burns the Mind.

He fortifi'd the double Gate,
And rarely thither came,
For, with one Spark of these, he streight
All Nature could inflame.

Till, by vicinity so long,
A nearer Way they sought;
And, grown magnetically strong,
Into each other wrought.

Thus all his fewel did unite
To make one fire high:
None ever burn'd so hot, so bright:
And Celia that am I.

So we alone the happy rest,
Whilst all the World is poor,
And have within our Selves possest
All Love's and Nature's store.

Eyes And Tears
How wisely Nature did decree,
With the same Eyes to weep and see!
That, having view'd the object vain,
They might be ready to complain.

And since the Self-deluding Sight,
In a false Angle takes each hight;
These Tears which better measure all,
Like wat'ry Lines and Plummets fall.

Two Tears, which Sorrow long did weigh
Within the Scales of either Eye,
And then paid out in equal Poise,
Are the true price of all my Joyes.

What in the World most fair appears,
Yea even Laughter, turns to Tears:
And all the Jewels which we prize,
Melt in these Pendants of the Eyes.

I have through every Garden been,
Amongst the Red,the White, the Green;
And yet, from all the flow'rs I saw,
No Hony, but these Tears could draw.

So the all-seeing Sun each day
Distills the World with Chymick Ray;
But finds the Essence only Showers,
Which straight in pity back he powers.

Yet happy they whom Grief doth bless,
That weep the more, and see the less:
And, to preserve their Sight more true,
Bath still their Eyes in their own Dew.

So Magdalen, in Tears more wise
Dissolv'd those captivating Eyes,
Whose liquid Chains could flowing meet
To fetter her Redeemers feet.

Not full sailes hasting loaden home,
Nor the chast Ladies pregnant Womb,
Nor Cynthia Teeming show's so fair,
As two Eyes swoln with weeping are.

The sparkling Glance that shoots Desire,
Drench'd in these Waves, does lose it fire.
Yea oft the Thund'rer pitty takes
And here the hissing Lightning slakes.

The Incense was to Heaven dear,
Not as a Perfume, but a Tear.
And Stars shew lovely in the Night,
But as they seem the Tears of Light.

Ope then mine Eyes your double Sluice,
And practise so your noblest Use.
For others too can see, or sleep;
But only humane Eyes can weep.

Now like two Clouds dissolving, drop,
And at each Tear in distance stop:
Now like two Fountains trickle down:
Now like two floods o'return and drown.

Thus let your Streams o'reflow your Springs,
Till Eyes and Tears be the same things:
And each the other's difference bears;
These weeping Eyes, those seeing Tears.

The Nymph Complaining For The Death Of Her Fawn
The wanton troopers riding by
Have shot my fawn, and it will die.
Ungentle men! They cannot thrive
To kill thee. Thou ne'er didst, alive,
Them any harm: alas nor could
Thy death yet do them any good.
I'm sure I never wished them ill,
Nor do I for all this; nor will:
But, if my simple pray'rs may yet
Prevail with Heaven to forget
Thy murder, I will join my tears
Rather than fail. But, O my fears!
It cannot die so. Heaven's King
Keeps register of every thing,
And nothing may we use in vain:
Ev'n beasts must be with justice slain,
Else men are made their deodands.
Though they should wash their guilty hands
In this warm life-blood, which doth part
From thine, and wound me to the heart,
Yet could they not be clean; their stain
Is dyed in such a purple grain.
There is not such another in
The world to offer for their sin.
Unconstant Sylvio, when yet
I had not found him counterfeit,
One morning (I remember well),
Tied in this silver chain and bell,
Gave it to me: nay and I know
What he said then -I'm sure I do.
Said he, "Look how your huntsman here
Hath taught a fawn to hunt his dear."
But Sylvio soon had me beguiled:
This waxed tame, while he grew wild,
And quite regardless of my smart,
Left me his fawn, but took his heart.
Thenceforth I set myself to play
My solitary time away,
With this: and very well content,
Could so mine idle life have spent.
For it was full of sport, and light
Of foot and heart; and did invite
Me to its game: it seemed to bless
Itself to me. How could I less
Than love it? O I cannot be
Unkind t' a beast that loveth me.
Had it lived long, I do not know
Whether it too might have done so

As Sylvio did: his gifts might be
Perhaps as false or more than he.
But I am sure, for aught that I
Could in so short a time espy,
Thy love was far more better then
The love of false and cruel men.
With sweetest milk and sugar first
I it at mine own fingers nursed.
And as it grew, so every day
It waxed more white and sweet than they.
It had so sweet a breath! And oft
I blushed to see its foot more soft
And white (shall I say?) than my hand
Nay, any lady's of the land!
It is a wond'rous thing how fleet
'Twas on those little silver feet;
With what a pretty skipping grace
It oft would challenge me the race;
And when 't had left me far away,
'Twould stay, and run again, and stay.
For it was nimbler much than hinds;
And trod as if on the four winds.
I have a garden of my own,
But so with roses overgrown
And lilies, that you would it guess
To be a little wilderness,
And all the spring-time of the year
It only loved to be there.
Among the beds of lilies I
Have sought it oft, where it should lie,
Yet could not, till itself would rise,
Find it, although before mine eyes;
For in the flaxen lilies' shade,
It like a bank of lilies laid.
Upon the roses it would feed,
Until its lips ev'n seemed to bleed:
And then to me 'twould boldly trip,
And print those roses on my lip.
But all its chief delight was still
On roses thus itself to fill,
And its pure virgin limbs to fold
In whitest sheets of lilies cold.
Had it lived long, it would have been
Lilies without, roses within.
O help! O help! I see it faint
And die as calmly as a saint!
See how it weeps! The tears do come
Sad, slowly dropping like a gum.
So weeps the wounded balsam; so
The holy frankincense doth flow;
The brotherless Heliades

Melt in such amber tears as these.
I in a golden vial will
Keep these two crystal tears; and fill
It till it do o'erflow with mine,
Then place it in Diana's shrine.
Now my sweet fawn is vanished to
Whither the swans and turtles go:
In fair Elysium to endure,
With milk-white lambs and ermins pure.
O do not run too fast, for I
Will but bespeak thy grave, and die.
First, my unhappy statue shall
Be cut in marble; and withal
Let it be weeping too: but there
Th' engraver sure his art may spare;
For I so truly thee bemoan
That I shall weep though I be stone,
Until my tears, still dropping, wear
My breast, themselves engraving there.
There at my feet shalt thou be laid,
Of purest alabaster made;
For I would have thine image be
White as I can, though not as thee.

Clorinda And Damon
Clorinda
Damon come drive thy flocks this way.

Damon
No : 'tis too late they went astray.

Clorinda
I have a grassy Scutcheon spy'd,
Where Flora blazons all her pride.
The grass I aim to feast thy Sheep :
The Flow'rs I for thy Temples keep.

Damon
Grass withers; and the Flow'rs too fade.

Clorinda
Seize the short Joyes then, ere they vade.
Seest thou that unfrequented Cave ?

Damon
That den?

Clorinda
Loves Shrine.

Damon
But Virtue's Grave.

Clorinda
In whose cool bosome we may lye
Safe from the Sun.

Damon
Not Heaven's Eye.

Clorinda
Near this, a Fountaines liquid Bell
Tinkles within the concave Shell.

Damon
Might a Soul bath there and be clean,
Or slake its Drought?

Clorinda
What is 't you mean?

Damon
These once had been enticing things,
Clorinda, Pastures, Caves, and Springs.

Clorinda
And what late change?

Damon
The other day
Pan met me.

Clorinda
What did great Pan say?

Damon
Words that transcend poor Shepherds skill,
But he ere since my Songs does fill:
And his Name swells my slender Oate.

Clorinda
Sweet must Pan sound in Damons Note.

Damon
Clorinda's voice might make it sweet.

Clorinda
Who would not in Pan's Praises meet ?

Chorus

Of Pan the flowry pastures sing,
Caves eccho and the Fountains ring.
Sing then while he doth us inspire;
For all the world is our Pan's Quire.

Damon The Mower
Heark how the Mower Damon Sung,
With love of Juliana stung!
While ev'ry thing did seem to paint
The Scene more fit for his complaint.
Like her fair Eyes the day was fair;
But scorching like his am'rous Care.
Sharp like his Sythe his Sorrow was,
And wither'd like his Hopes the Grass.

Oh what unusual Heats are here,
Which thus our Sun-burn'd Meadows sear!
The Grass-hopper its pipe gives ore;
And hamstring'd Frogs can dance no more.
But in the brook the green Frog wades;
And Grass-hoppers seek out the shades.
Only the Snake, that kept within,
Now glitters in its second skin.

This heat the Sun could never raise,
Nor Dog-star so inflame's the dayes.
It from an higher Beauty grow'th,
Which burns the Fields and Mower both:
Which made the Dog, and makes the Sun
Hotter then his own Phaeton.
Not July causeth these Extremes,
But Juliana's scorching beams.

Tell me where I may pass the Fires
Of the hot day, or hot desires.
To what cool Cave shall I descend,
Or to what gelid Fountain bend?
Alas! I look for Ease in vain,
When Remedies themselves complain.
No moisture but my Tears do rest,
Nor Cold but in her Icy Breast.

How long wilt Thou, fair Shepheardess,
Esteem me, and my Presents less?
To Thee the harmless Snake I bring,
Disarmed of its teeth and sting.
To Thee Chameleons changing-hue,
And Oak leaves tipt with hony due.
Yet Thou ungrateful hast not sought

Nor what they are, nor who them brought.

I am the Mower Damon, known
Through all the Meadows I have mown.
On me the Morn her dew distills
Before her darling Daffadils.
And, if at Noon my toil me heat,
The Sun himself licks off my Sweat.
While, going home, the Ev'ning sweet
In cowslip-water bathes my feet.

What, though the piping Shepherd stock
The plains with an unnum'red Flock,
This Sithe of mine discovers wide
More ground then all his Sheep do hide.
With this the golden fleece I shear
Of all these Closes ev'ry Year.
And though in Wooll more poor then they,
Yet am I richer far in Hay.

Nor am I so deform'd to sight,
If in my Sithe I looked right;
In which I see my Picture done,
As in a crescent Moon the Sun.
The deathless Fairyes take me oft
To lead them in their Danses soft:
And, when I tune my self to sing,
About me they contract their Ring.

How happy might I still have mow'd,
Had not Love here his Thistles sow'd!
But now I all the day complain,
Joyning my Labour to my Pain;
And with my Sythe cut down the Grass,
Yet still my Grief is where it was:
But, when the Iron blunter grows,
Sighing I whet my Sythe and Woes.

While thus he threw his Elbow round,
Depopulating all the Ground,
And, with his whistling Sythe, does cut
Each stroke between the Earth and Root,
The edged Stele by careless chance
Did into his own Ankle glance;
And there among the Grass fell down,
By his own Sythe, the Mower mown.

Alas! said He, these hurts are slight
To those that dye by Loves despight.
With Shepherds-purse, and Clowns-all-heal,
The Blood I stanch, and Wound I seal.

Only for him no Cure is found,
Whom Julianas Eyes do wound.
'Tis death alone that this must do:
For Death thou art a Mower too.

The Mower's Song
My Mind was once the true survey
Of all these Medows fresh and gay;
And in the greenness of the Grass
Did see its Hopes as in a Glass;
When Juliana came, and she
What I do to the Grass, does to my Thoughts and Me.

But these, while I with Sorrow pine,
Grew more luxuriant still and fine;
That not one Blade of Grass you spy'd,
But had a Flower on either side;
When Juliana came, and She
What I do to the Grass, does to my Thoughts and Me.

Unthankful Meadows, could you so
A fellowship so true forego,
And in your gawdy May-games meet,
While I lay trodden under feet?
When Juliana came , and She
What I do to the Grass, does to my Thoughts and Me.

But what you in Compassion ought,
Shall now by my Revenge be wrought:
And Flow'rs, and Grass, and I and all,
Will in one common Ruine fall.
For Juliana comes, and She
What I do to the Grass, does to my Thoughts and Me.

And thus, ye Meadows, which have been
Companions of my thoughts more green,
Shall now the Heraldry become
With which I shall adorn my Tomb;
For Juliana comes, and She
What I do to the Grass, does to my Thoughts and Me.

The Mower To The Glow Worms
Ye living lamps, by whose dear light
The nightingale does sit so late,
And studying all the summer night,
Her matchless songs does meditate;

Ye county comets, that portend
No war nor prince's funeral,
Shining unto no higher end
Than to presage the grass's fall;

Ye glow-worms, whose officious flame
To wand'ring mowers shows the way,
That in the night have lost their aim,
And after foolish fires do stray;

Your courteous lights in vain you waste,
Since Juliana here is come,
For she my mind hath so displac'd
That I shall never find my home.

The Mower Against Gardens
Luxurious Man, to bring his Vice in use,
Did after him the World seduce:
And from the Fields the Flow'rs and Plants allure,
Where Nature was most plain and pure.
He first enclos'd within the Gardens square
A dead and standing pool of Air:
And a more luscious Earth for them did knead,
Which stupifi'd them while it fed.
The Pink grew then as double as his Mind;
The nutriment did change the kind.
With strange perfumes he did the Roses taint.
And Flow'rs themselves were taught to paint.
The Tulip, white, did for complexion seek;
And learn'd to interline its cheek:
Its Onion root they then so high did hold,
That one was for a Meadow sold.
Another World was search'd, through Oceans new,
To find the Marvel Of Peru.
And yet these Rarities might be allow'd,
To Man, that Sov'raign thing and proud;
Had he not dealt between the Bark and Tree,
Forbidden mixtures there to see.
No Plant now knew the Stock from which it came;
He grafts upon the Wild the Tame:
That the uncertain and adult'rate fruit
Might put the Palate in dispute.
His green Seraglio has its Eunuchs too;
Lest any Tyrant him out-doe.
And in the Cherry he does Nature vex,
To procreate without a Sex.
'Tis all enforc'd; the Fountain and the Grot;
While the sweet Fields do lye forgot:
Where willing Nature does to all dispence

A wild and fragrant Innocence:
And Fauns and Faryes do the Meadows till,
More by their presence then their skill.
Their Statues polish'd by some ancient hand,
May to adorn the Gardens stand:
But howso'ere the Figures do excel,
The Gods themselves with us do dwell.

The Picture Of Little T. C. In A Prospect Of Flowers
See with what simplicity
This nymph begins her golden days!
In the green grass she loves to lie,
And there with her fair aspect tames
The wilder flowers, and gives them names;
But only with the roses plays,
And them does tell
What colour best becomes them, and what smell.

Who can foretell for what high cause
This darling of the gods was born?
Yet this is she whose chaster laws
The wanton Love shall one day fear,
And, under her command severe,
See his bow broke and ensigns torn.
Happy who can
Appease this virtuous enemy of man!

O then let me in time compound
And parley with those conquering eyes,
Ere they have tried their force to wound;
Ere with their glancing wheels they drive
In triumph over hearts that strive,
And them that yield but more despise:
Let me be laid,
Where I may see the glories from some shade.

Meantime, whilst every verdant thing
Itself does at thy beauty charm,
Reform the errors of the Spring;
Make that the tulips may have share
Of sweetness, seeing they are fair,
And roses of their thorns disarm;
But most procure
That violets may a longer age endure.

But O, young beauty of the woods,
Whom Nature courts with fruits and flowers,
Gather the flowers, but spare the buds;
Lest Flora, angry at thy crime

To kill her infants in their prime,
Do quickly make th' example yours;
And ere we see,
Nip in the blossom all our hopes and thee.

Thoughts In A Garden
How vainly men themselves amaze
To win the palm, the oak, or bays,
And their uncessant labours see
Crown'd from some single herb or tree,
Whose short and narrow-verged shade
Does prudently their toils upbraid;
While all the flowers and trees do close
To weave the garlands of repose!

Fair Quiet, have I found thee here,
And Innocence thy sister dear?
Mistaken long, I sought you then
In busy companies of men:
Your sacred plants, if here below,
Only among the plants will grow:
Society is all but rude
To this delicious solitude.

No white nor red was ever seen
So amorous as this lovely green.
Fond lovers, cruel as their flame,
Cut in these trees their mistress' name:
Little, alas! they know or heed
How far these beauties hers exceed!
Fair trees! wheres'e'er your barks I wound,
No name shall but your own be found.

When we have run our passions' heat,
Love hither makes his best retreat:
The gods, that mortal beauty chase,
Still in a tree did end their race;
Apollo hunted Daphne so
Only that she might laurel grow;
And Pan did after Syrinx speed
Not as a nymph, but for a reed.

What wondrous life in this I lead!
Ripe apples drop about my head;
The luscious clusters of the vine
Upon my mouth do crush their wine;
The nectarine and curious peach
Into my hands themselves do reach;
Stumbling on melons, as I pass,

Ensnared with flowers, I fall on grass.

Meanwhile the mind from pleasure less
Withdraws into its happiness;
The mind, that ocean where each kind
Does straight its own resemblance find;
Yet it creates, transcending these,
Far other worlds, and other seas;
Annihilating all that's made
To a green thought in a green shade.

Here at the fountain's sliding foot,
Or at some fruit-tree's mossy root,
Casting the body's vest aside,
My soul into the boughs does glide;
There, like a bird, it sits and sings,
Then whets and combs its silver wings,
And, till prepared for longer flight,
Waves in its plumes the various light.

Such was that happy Garden-state
While man there walk'd without a mate:
After a place so pure and sweet,
What other help could yet be meet!
But 'twas beyond a mortal's share
To wander solitary there:
Two paradises 'twere in one,
To live in Paradise alone.

How well the skilful gard'ner drew
Of flowers and herbs this dial new!
Where, from above, the milder sun
Does through a fragrant zodiac run:
And, as it works, th' industrious bee
Computes its time as well as we.
How could such sweet and wholesome hours
Be reckon'd, but with herbs and flowers!

A Dialogue Between Thyrsis And Dorinda
Dorinda
When Death, shall snatch us from these Kids,
And shut up our divided Lids,
Tell me Thyrsis, prethee do,
Whither thou and I must go.

Thyrsis
To the Elizium: (Dorinda) oh where i'st?

Thyrsis

A Chast Soul, can never mis't.

Dorinda
I know no way, but one, our home
Is our Elizium?

Thyrsis
Cast thine Eye to yonder Skie,
There the milky way doth lye;
'Tis a sure but rugged way,
That leads to Everlasting day.

Dorinda
There Birds may nest, but how can I,
That have no wings and cannot fly.

Thyrsis
Do not sigh (fair Nimph) for fire
Hath no wings, yet doth aspire
Till it hit, against the pole,
Heaven's the Center of the Soul.

Dorinda
But in Elizium how do they
Pass Eternity away.

Thyrsis
Ho, ther's, neither hope nor fear
Ther's no Wolf, no Fox, no Bear.
No need of Dog to fetch our stray,
Our Lightfoot we may give away;
And there most sweetly thine Ear
May feast with Musick of the Sphear.
How I my future state
By silent thinking, Antidate:
I preethe let us spend, our time come,
In talking of Elizium.

Thyrsis
Then I'le go on: There, sheep are full
Of softest grass, and softest wooll;
There, birds sing Consorts, garlands grow,
Cold winds do whisper,springs do flow.
There, always is, a rising Sun,
And day is ever, but begun.
Shepheards there, bear equal sway,
And every Nimph's a Queen of May.

Dorinda
Ah me, ah me.

Thyrsis
Dorinda, why do'st Cry?

Dorinda
I'm sick, I'm sick, and fain would dye:
Convinc't me now, that this is true,
By bidding, with mee, all adieu
I cannot live, without thee, I
Will for thee,much more with thee dye.

Dorinda
Then let us give Corellia charge o'th Sheep,
And thou and I'le pick poppies and them steep
In wine, and drink on't even till we weep,
So shall we smoothly pass away in sleep.

The Unfortunate Lover
Alas, how pleasant are their dayes
With whom the Infant Love yet playes!
Sorted by pairs, they still are seen
By Fountains cool, and Shadows green.
But soon these Flames do lose their light,
Like Meteors of a Summers night:
Nor can they to that Region climb,
To make impression upon Time.

'Twas in a Shipwrack, when the Seas
Rul'd, and the Winds did what they please,
That my poor Lover floting lay,
And, e're brought forth, was cast away:
Till at the last the master-Wave.
Upon the Rock his Mother drave;
And there she split against the Stone,
In a Cesarian Section.

The Sea him lent these bitter Tears
Which at his Eyes he alwaies bears.
And from the Winds the Sighs he bore,
Which through his surging Breast do roar.
No Day he saw but that which breaks,
Through frighted Clouds in forked streaks.
While round the ratling Thunder hurl'd,
As at the Fun'ral of the World.

While Nature to his Birth presents
This masque of quarrelling Elements;
A num'rous fleet of Corm'rants black,
That sail'd insulting o're the Wrack,
Receiv'd into their cruel Care,

Th' unfortunate and abject Heir:
Guardians most fit to entertain
The Orphan of the Hurricane.

They fed him up with Hopes and Air,
Which soon digested to Despair.
And as one Corm'rant fed him, still
Another on his Heart did bill.
Thus while they famish him, and feast,
He both consumed, and increast:
And languished with doubtful Breath,
Th' Amphibium of Life and Death.

And now, when angry Heaven wou'd
Behold a spectacle of Blood,
Fortune and He are call'd to play
At sharp before it all the day:
And Tyrant Love his brest does ply
With all his wing'd Artillery.
Whilst he, betwixt the Flames and Waves,
Like Ajax, the mad Tempest braves.

See how he nak'd and fierce does stand,
Cuffing the Thunder with one hand;
While with the other he does lock,
And grapple, with the stubborn Rock:
From which he with each Wave rebounds,
Torn into Flames, and ragg'd with Wounds.
And all he saies, a Lover drest
In his own Blood does relish best.

This is the only Banneret
That ever Love created yet:
Who though, by the Malignant Starrs,
Forced to live in Storms and Warrs;
Yet dying leaves a Perfume here,
And Musick within every Ear:
And he in Story only rules,
In a Field Sable a Lover Gules.

Last Instructions To A Painter
After two sittings, now our Lady State
To end her picture does the third time wait.
But ere thou fall'st to work, first, Painter, see
If't ben't too slight grown or too hard for thee.
Canst thou paint without colors? Then 'tis right:
For so we too without a fleet can fight.
Or canst thou daub a signpost, and that ill?
'Twill suit our great debauch and little skill.
Or hast thou marked how antic masters limn

On opp'site points, the black against the white.
Those having lost the nation at tric-trac,
These now adventuring how to win it back.
The dice betwixt them must the fate divide
(As chance doth still in multitudes decide).
But here the Court does its advantage know,
For the cheat Turner for them both must throw.
As some from boxes, he so from the chair
Can strike the die and still with them goes share.

Here, Painter, rest a little, and survey
With what small arts the public game they play.
For so too Rubens, with affairs of state,
His labouring pencil oft would recreate.

The close Cabal marked how the Navy eats,
And thought all lost that goes not to the cheats,
So therefore secretly for peace decrees,
Yet as for war the Parliament should squeeze,
And fix to the revénue such a sum
Should Goodrick silence and strike Paston dumb,
Should pay land armies, should dissolve the vain
Commons, and ever such a court maintain;
Hyde's avarice, Bennet's luxury should suffice,
And what can these defray but the Excise?
Excise a monster worse than e'er before
Frighted the midwife and the mother tore.
A thousand hands she has and thousand eyes,
Breaks into shops and into cellars pries,
And on all trade like cassowar she feeds:
Chops off the piece wheres'e'er she close the jaw,
Else swallows all down her indented maw.
She stalks all day in streets concealed from sight
And flies, like bats with leathern wings, by night;
She wastes the country and on cities preys.
Her, of a female harpy, in dog days,
Black Birch, of all the earth-born race most hot
And most rapacious, like himself, begot,
And, of his brat enamoured, as't increased,
Buggered in incest with the mongrel beast.

Say, Muse, for nothing can escape thy sight
(And, Painter, wanting other, draw this fight),
Who, in an English senate, fierce debate
Could raise so long for this new whore of state.

Of early wittols first the troop marched in
For diligence renowned and discipline
In loyal haste they left young wives in bed,
And Denham these by one consent did head.
Of the old courtiers, next a squadron came,

That sold their master, led by Ashburnham.
To them succeeds a desipicable rout,
But know the word and well could face about;
Expectants pale, with hopes of spoil allured,
Though yet but pioneers, and led by Stew'rd.
Then damning cowards ranged the vocal plain,
Wood these command, the Knight of the Horn and Cane.
Still his hook-shoulder seems the blow to dread,
And under's armpit he defends his head.
The posture strange men laughed at of his poll,
Hid with his elbow like the spice he stole.
Headless St Denys so his head does bear,
And both of them alike French martyrs were.
Court officers, as used, the next place took,
And followed, Fox, but with disdainful look.
His birth, his youth, his brokage all dispraise
In vain, for always he commands that pays.
Then the procurers under Progers filed
Gentlest of men and his lieutenant mild,
Brounker, Love's squire, through all the field arrayed,
No troop was better clad, nor so well paid.
Then marched the troop of Clarendon, all full
Haters of fowl, to teal preferring bull:
Gross bodies, grosser minds, and grossest cheats,
And bloated Wren conducts them to their seats.
Charlton advances next, whose coif does awe
The Mitre troop, and with his looks gives law.
He marched with beaver cocked of bishop's brim,
And hid much fraud under an aspect grim.
Next the lawyers' merecenary band appear:
Finch in the front, and Thurland in the rear.
The troop of privilege, a rabble bare
Of debtors deep, fell to Trelawney's care.
Their fortune's error they supplied in rage,
Nor any further would than these engage.
Then marched the troop, whose valiant acts before
(Their public acts) obliged them still to more.
For chimney's sake they all Sir Pool obeyed,
Or in his absence him that first it laid.
Then comes the thrifty troop of privateers,
Whose horses each with other interfered.
Before them Higgons rides with brow compact,
Mourning his Countess, anxious for his Act.
Sir Frederick and Sir Solomon draw lots
For the command of politics or sots,
Thence fell to words, but quarrel to adjourn;
Their friends agreed they should command by turn.
Carteret the rich did the accountants guide
And in ill English all the world defied.
The Papists, but of these the House had none
Else Talbot offered to have led them on.

Bold Duncombe next, of the projectors chief,
And old Fitz-harding of the Eaters Beef.
Late and disordered out the drinkers drew,
Scarce them their leaders, they their leaders knew.
Before them entered, equal in command,
Apsley and Brod'rick, marching hand in hand.
Last then but one, Powell that could not ride,
Led the French standard, weltering in his stride.
He, to excuse his slowness, truth confessed
That 'twas so long before he could be dressed.
The Lord's sons, last, all these did reinforce:
Cornb'ry before them managed hobby-horse.

Never before nor since, an host so steeled
Trooped on to muster in the Tothill Field:
Not the first cock-horse that with cork were shod
To rescue Albemarle from the sea-cod,
Nor the late feather-men, whom Tomkins fierce
Shall with one breath, like thistledown disperse.
All the two Coventrys their generals chose
For one had much, the other nought to lose;
Nor better choice all accidents could hit,
While Hector Harry steers by Will the Wit.
They both accept the charge with merry glee,
To fight a battle, from all gunshot free.
Pleased with their numbers, yet in valour wise,
They feign a parley, better to surprise;
They that ere long shall the rude Dutch upbraid,
Who in the time of treaty durst invade.

Thick was the morning, and the House was thin,
The Speaker early, when they all fell in.
Propitious heavens, had not you them crossed,
Excise had got the day, and all been lost.
For the other side all in loose quarters lay,
Without intelligence, command, or pay:
A scattered body, which the foe ne'er tried,
But oftener did among themselves divide.
And some ran o'er each night, while others sleep,
And undescried returned ere morning peep.
But Strangeways, that all night still walked the round
(For vigilance and courage both renowned)
First spied he enemy and gave the 'larm,
Fighting it single till the rest might arm.
Such Romand Cocles strid before the foe,
The falling bridge behind, the stream below.

Each ran, as chance him guides to several post,
And all to pattern his example boast.
Their former trophies they recall to mind
And to new edge their angry courage grind.

First entered forward Temple, conqueror
Of Irish cattle and Solicitor;
Then daring Seymour, that with spear and shield
Had stretched the Monster Patent on the field;
Keen Whorwood next, in aid of damsel frail,
That pierced the giant Mordaunt through his mail;
And surly Williams, the accountants' bane;
And Lovelace young, of chimney-men the cane.
Old Waller, trumpet-general, swore he'd write
This combat truer than the naval fight.
How'rd on's birth, wit, strength, courage much presumes
And in his breast wears many Montezumes.
These and some more with single valour stay
The adverse troops, and hold them all at bay.
Each thinks his person represents the whole,
And with that thought does multiply his soul,
Believes himself an army, theirs, one man
As easily conquered, and believing can,
With heart of bees so full, and head of mites,
That each, though duelling, a battle fights.
Such once Orlando, famous in romance,
Broached whole brigades like larks upon his lance.

But strength at last still under number bows,
And the faint sweat trickled down Temple's brows.
E'en iron Strangeways, chafing, yet gave back,
Spent with fatigue, to breathe a while toback.
When marching in, a seasonable recruit
Of citizens and merchants held dispute;
And, charging all their pikes, a sullen band
Of Presyterian Switzers made a stand.

Nor could all these the field have long maintained
But for th' unknown reserve that still remained:
A gross of English gentry, nobly born,
Of clear estates, and to no faction sworn,
Dear lovers of their king, and death to meet
For country's cause, that glorious think and sweet;
To speak not forward, but in action brave,
In giving generous, but in counsel grave;
Candidly credulous for once, nay twice,
But sure the Devil cannot cheat them thrice.
The van and battle, though retiring, falls
Without dosorder in their intervals.
Then, closing all in equal front, fall on,
Led by great Garway and great Littleton.
Lee, ready to obey or to command,
Adjutant-general, was still at hand.
The martial standard, Sandys displaying, shows
St Dunstan in it, tweaking Satan's nose.
See sudden chance of war! To paint or write

Is longer work and harder than to fight.
At the first charge the enemy give out,
And the Excise receives a total rout.

Broken in courage, yet the men the same
Resolve henceforth upon their other game:
Where force had failed, with stratagem to play,
And what haste lost, recover by delay.
St Albans straight is sent to, to forbear,
Lest the sure peace, forsooth, too soon appear.
The seamen's clamour to three ends they use:
To cheat their pay, feign want, the House accuse.
Each day they bring the tale, and that too true,
How strong the Dutch their equipage renew.
Meantime through all the yards their orders run
To lay the ships up, cease the keels begun.
The timber rots, and useless axe doth rust,
Th' unpracticed saw lies buried in its dust,
The busy hammer sleeps, the ropes untwine,
The stores and wages all are mine and thine.
Along the coast and harbours they make care
That money lack, nor forts be in repair.
Long thus they could against the House conspire,
Load them with envy, and with sitting tire.
And the loved King, and never yet denied,
Is brought to beg in public and to chide;
But when this failed, and months enow were spent,
They with the first day's proffer seem content,
And to Land-Tax from the Excise turn round,
Bought off with eighteen-hundred-thousand pound.
Thus like fair theives, the Commons' purse they share,
But all the members' lives, consulting, spare.

Blither than hare that hath escaped the hounds,
The House prorogued, the Chancellor rebounds.
Not so decrepit Aeson, hashed and stewed,
With bitter herbs, rose from the pot renewed,
And with fresh age felt his glad limbs unite;
His gout (yet still he cursed) had left him quite.
What frosts to fruit, what arsenic to the rat,
What to fair Denham, mortal chocolate,
What an account to Carteret, that, and more,
A Parliament is to the Chancellor.
So the Sad-tree shrinks from the morning's eye,
But blooms all night and shoots its branches high.
So, at the sun's recess, again returns
The comet dread, and earth and heaven burns.

Now Mordaunt may, within his castle tower,
Imprison parents, and the child deflower.
The Irish herd is now let loose and comes

By millions over, not by hecatombs;
And now, now the Canary Patent may
Be broached again for the great holiday.

See how he reigns in his new palace culminant,
And sits in state divine like Jove the fulminant!
First Buckingham, that durst to him rebel,
Blasted with lightning, struck wtih thunder, fell.
Next the twelve Commons are condemned to groan
And roll in vain at Sisyphus's stone.
But still he cared, while in revenge he braved
That peace secured and money might be saved:
Gain and revenge, revenge and gain are sweet
United most, else when by turns they meet.
France had St Albans promised (so they sing),
St Albans promised him, and he the King:
The Count forthwith is ordered all to close,
To play for Flanders and the stake to lose,
While, chained together, two ambassadors
Like slaves shall beg for peace at Holland's doors.
This done, among his Cyclops he retires
To forge new thunder and inspect their fires.

The court as once of war, now fond of peace,
All to new sports their wanton fears release.
From Greenwich (where intelligence they hold)
Comes news of pastime martial and old,
A punishment invented first to awe
Masculine wives transgressing Nature's law,
Where, when the brawny female disobeys,
And beats the husband till for peace he prays,
No concerned jury for him damage finds,
Nor partial justice her behavior binds,
But the just street does the next house invade,
Mounting the neighbour couple on lean jade,
The distaff knocks, the grains from kettle fly,
And boys and girls in troops run hooting by:
Prudent antiquity, that knew by shame,
Better than law, domestic crimes to tame,
And taught youth by spectácle innocent!
So thou and I, dear Painter, represent
In quick effigy, others' faults, and feign
By making them ridiculous, to restrain.
With homely sight they chose thus to relax
The joys of state, for the new Peace and Tax.
So Holland with us had the mastery tried,
And our next neighbours, France and Flanders, ride.

But a fresh news the great designment nips,
Of, at the Isle of Candy, Dutch and ships!
Bab May and Arlington did wisely scoff

And thought all safe, if they were so far off.
Modern geographers, 'twas there, they thought,
Where Venice twenty years the Turk had fought,
While the first year our navy is but shown,
The next divided, and the third we've none.
They, by the name, mistook it for that isle
Where Pilgrim Palmer travelled in exile
With the bull's horn to measure his own head
And on Pasiphaë's tomb to drop a bead.
But Morice learn'd demónstrates, by the post,
This Isle of Candy was on Essex' coast.

Fresh messengers still the sad news assure;
More timorous now we are than first secure.
False terrors our believing fears devise,
And the French army one from Calais spies.
Bennet and May and those of shorter reach
Change all for guineas, and a crown for each,
But wiser men and well foreseen in chance
In Holland theirs had lodged before, and France.
Whitehall's unsafe; the court all meditates
To fly to Windsor and mure up the gates.
Each does the other blame, and all distrust;
(That Mordaunt, new obliged, would sure be just.)
Not such a fatal stupefaction reigned
At London's flame, nor so the court complained.
The Bloodworth_Chancellor gives, then does recall
Orders; amazed, at last gives none at all.

St Alban's writ to, that he may bewail
To Master Louis, and tell coward tale
How yet the Hollanders do make a noise,
Threaten to beat us, and are naughty boys.
Now Dolman's dosobedient, and they still
Uncivil; his unkindness would us kill.
Tell him our ships unrigged, our forts unmanned,
Our money spent; else 'twere at his command.
Summon him therefore of his word and prove
To move him out of pity, if not love;
Pray him to make De Witt and Ruyter cease,
And whip the Dutch unless they'll hold their peace.
But Louis was of memory but dull
And to St Albans too undutiful,
Nor word nor near relation did revere,
But asked him bluntly for his character.
The gravelled Count did with the answer faint
His character was that which thou didst paint
Trusses his baggage and the camp does fly.
Yet Louis writes and, lest our heart should break,
Consoles us morally out of Seneque.

Two letters next unto Breda are sent:
In cipher one to Harry Excellent;
The first instructs our (verse the name abhors)
Plenipotentiary ambassadors
To prove by Scripture treaty does imply
Cessation, as the look adultery,
And that, by law of arms, in martial strife,
Who yields his sword has title to his life.
Presbyter Holles the first point should clear,
The second Coventry the Cavalier;
But, whould they not be argued back from sea,
Then to return home straight, infecta re.
But Harry's ordered, if they won't recall
Their fleet, to threaten, we will grant them all.
The Dutch are then in proclamation shent
For sin against th' eleventh commandment.
Hyde's flippant style there pleasantly curvets,
Still his sharp wit on states and princes whets
(So Spain could not escape his laughter's spleen:
None but himsef must choose the King a Queen),
But when he came the odious clause to pen
That summons up the Parliament again,
His writing master many a time he banned
And wished himself the gout to seize his hand.
Never old lecher more repugnance felt,
Consenting, for his rupture, to be gelt;
But still then hope him solaced, ere they come,
To work the peace and so to send them home,
Or in their hasty call to find a flaw,
Their acts to vitiate, and them overawe;
But most relied upon this Dutch pretence
To raise a two-endged army for's defence.

First then he marched our whole militia's force
(As if indeed we ships or Dutch had horse);
Then from the usual commonplace, he blames
These, and in standing army's praise declaims;
And the wise court that always loved it dear,
Now thinks all but too little for their fear.
Hyde stamps, and straight upon the ground the swarms
Of current Myrmidons appear in arms,
And for their pay he writes, as from the King
With that cursed quill plucked from a vulture's wing
Of the whole nation now to ask a loan
(The eighteen-hundred-thousand pound was gone).

This done, he pens a proclamation stout,
In rescue of the banquiers banquerout,
His minion imps that, in his secret part,
Lie nuzzling at the sacremental wart,
Horse-leeches circling at the hem'rrhoid vein:

He sucks the King, they him, he them again.
The kingdom's farm he lets to them bid least
(Greater the bribe, and that's at interest).
Here men, induced by safety, gain, and ease,
Their money lodge; confiscate when he please.
These can at need, at instant, with a scrip
(This liked him best) his cash beyond sea whip.
When Dutch invade, when Parliament prepare,
How can he engines so convenient spare?
Let no man touch them or demand his own,
Pain of displeasure of great Clarendon.

The state affairs thus marshalled, for the rest
Monck in his shirt against the Dutch is pressed.
Often, dear Painter, have I sat and mused
Why he should still be 'n all adventures used,
If they for nothing ill, like ashen wood,
Or think him, like Herb John for nothing good;
Whether his valour they so much admire,
Or that for cowardice they all retire,
As heaven in storms, they call in gusts of state
On Monck and Parliament, yet both do hate.
All causes sure concur, but most they think
Under Hercúlean labours he may sink.
Soon then the independent troops would close,
And Hyde's last project would his place dispose.

Ruyter the while, that had our ocean curbed,
Sailed now among our rivers undistrubed,
Surveyed their crystal streams and banks so green
And beauties ere this never naked seen.
Through the vain sedge, the bashful nymphs he eyed:
Bosoms, and all which from themselves they hide.
The sun much brighter, and the skies more clear,
He finds the air and all things sweeter here.
The sudden change, and such a tempting sight
Swells his old veins with fresh blood, fresh delight.
Like am'rous victors he begins to shave,
And his new face looks in the English wave.
His sporting navy all about him swim
And witness their complacence in their trim.
Their streaming silks play through the weather fair
And with inveigling colours court the air,
While the red flags breathe on their topmasts high
Terror and war, but want an enemy.
Among the shrouds the seamen sit and sing,
And wanton boys on every rope do cling.
Old Neptune springs the tides and water lent
(The gods themselves do help the provident),
And where the deep keel on the shallow cleaves,
With trident's lever, and great shoulder heaves.

&Aelig;olus their sails inspires with eastern wind,
Puffs them along, and breathes upon them kind.
With pearly shell the Tritons all the while
Sound the sea-march and guide to Sheppey Isle.

So I have seen in April's bud arise
A fleet of clouds, sailing along the skies;
The liquid region with their squadrons filled,
Their airy sterns the sun behind does gild;
And gentle gales them steer, and heaven drives,
When, all on sudden, their calm bosom rives
With thunder and lightning from each armèd cloud;
Shepherds themselves in vain in bushes shroud.
Such up the stream the Belgic navy glides
And at Sheerness unloads its stormy sides.

Spragge there, though practised in the sea command,
With panting heart lay like a fish on land
And quickly judged the fort was not tenáble
Which, if a house, yet were not tenantáble
No man can sit there safe: the cannon pours
Thorough the walls untight and bullet showers,
The neighbourhood ill, and an unwholesome seat,
So at the first salute resolves retreat,
And swore that he would never more dwell there
Until the city put it in repair.
So he in front, his garrison in rear,
March straight to Chatham to increase the fear.

There our sick ships unrigged in summer lay
Like moulting fowl, a weak and easy prey,
For whose strong bulk earth scarce could timber find,
The ocean water, or the heavens wind
Those oaken giants of the ancient race,
That ruled all seas and did our Channel grace.
The conscious stag so, once the forest's dread,
Flies to the wood and hides his armless head.
Ruyter forthwith a squadron does untack;
They sail securely through the river's track.
An English pilot too (O shame, O sin!)
Cheated of pay, was he that showed them in.
Our wretched ships within their fate attend,
And all our hopes now on frail chain depend:
(Engine so slight to guard us from the sea,
It fitter seemed to captivate a flea).
A skipper rude shocks it without respect,
Filling his sails more force to re-collect.
Th' English from shore the iron deaf invoke
For its last aid: `Hold chain, or we are broke.'
But with her sailing weight, the Holland keel,
Snapping the brittle links, does thorough reel,

And to the rest the opened passage show;
Monck from the bank the dismal sight does view.
Our feathered gallants, which came down that day
To be spectators safe of the new play,
Leave him alone when first they hear the gun
(Cornb'ry the fleetest) and to London run.
Our seamen, whom no danger's shape could fright,
Unpaid, refuse to mount our ships for spite,
Or to their fellows swim on board the Dutch,
Which show the tempting metal in their clutch.
Oft had he sent of Duncombe and of Legge
Cannon and powder, but in vain, to beg;
And Upnor Castle's ill-deserted wall,
Now needful, does for ammunition call.
He finds, wheres'e'er he succor might expect,
Confusion, folly, treach'ry, fear, neglect.
But when the Royal Charles (what rage, what grief)
He saw seized, and could give her no relief!
That sacred keel which had, as he, restored
His exiled sovereign on its happy board,
And thence the British Admiral became,
Crowned, for that merit, with their master's name;
That pleasure-boat of war, in whose dear side
Secure so oft he had this foe defied,
Now a cheap spoil, and the mean victor's slave,
Taught the Dutch colours from its top to wave;
Of former glories the reproachful thought
With present shame compared, his mind destraught.
Such from Euphrates' bank, a tigress fell
After the robber for her whelps doth yell;
But sees enraged the river flow between,
Frustrate revenge and love, by loss more keen,
At her own breast her useless claws does arm:
She tears herself, since him she cannot harm.

The guards, placed for the chain's and fleet's defence,
Long since were fled on many a feigned pretence.
Daniel had there adventured, man of might,
Sweet Painter, draw his picture while I write.
Paint him of person tall, and big of bone,
Large limbs like ox, not to be killed but shown.
Scarce can burnt ivory feign an hair so black,
Or face so red, thine ocher and thy lac.
Mix a vain terror in his martial look,
And all those lines by which men are mistook;
But when, by shame constrained to go on board,
He heard how the wild cannon nearer roared,
And saw himself confined like sheep in pen,
Daniel then thought he was in lion's den.
And when the frightful fireships he saw,
Pregnant with sulphur, to him nearer draw,

Captain, lieutenant, ensign, all make haste
Ere in the fiery furnace they be cast
Three children tall, unsinged, away they row,
Like Shadrack, Meschack, and Abednego.

Not so brave Douglas, on whose lovely chin
The early down but newly did begin,
And modest beauty yet his sex did veil,
While envious virgins hope he is a male.
His yellow locks curl back themselves to seek,
Nor other courtship knew but to his cheek.
Oft, as he in chill Esk or Seine by night
Hardened and cooled his limbs, so soft, so white,
Among the reeds, to be espied by him,
The nymphs would rustle; he would forward swim.
They sighed and said, `Fond boy, why so untame
That fliest love's fires, reserved for other flame?'
Fixed on his ship, he faced that horrid day
And wondered much at those that ran away.
Nor other fear himself could comprehend
Then, lest heaven fall ere thither he ascend,
But entertains the while his time too short
With birding at the Dutch, as if in sport,
Or waves his sword, and could he them conjúre
Within its circle, knows himself secure.
The fatal bark him boards with grappling fire,
And safely through its port the Dutch retire.
That precious life he yet disdains to save
Or with known art to try the gentle wave.
Much him the honours of his ancient race
Inspire, nor would he his own deeds deface,
And secret joy in his calm soul does rise
That Monck looks on to see how Douglas dies.
Like a glad lover, the fierce flames he meets,
And tries his first embraces in their sheets.
His shape exact, which the bright flames enfold,
Like the sun's statue stands of burnished gold.
Round the transparent fire about him flows,
As the clear amber on the bee does close,
And, as on angels' heads their glories shine,
His burning locks adorn his face divine.
But when in this immortal mind he felt
His altering form and soldered limbs to melt,
Down on the deck he laid himself and died,
With his dear sword reposing by his side,
And on the flaming plank, so rests his head
As one that's warmed himself and gone to bed.
His ship burns down, and with his relics sinks,
And the sad stream beneath his ashes drinks.
Fortunate boy, if either pencil's fame,
Or if my verse can propagate thy name,

When Oeta and Alcides are forgot,
Our English youth shall sing the valiant Scot.

Each doleful day still with fresh loss returns:
The Loyal London now the third time burns,
And the true Royal Oak and Royal James,
Allied in fate, increase, with theirs, her flames.
Of all our navy none should now survive,
But that the ships themselves were taught to dive,
And the kind river in its creek them hides,
Fraughting their piercèd keels with oozy tides.

Up to the bridge contagious terror struck:
The Tower itself with the near danger shook,
And were not Ruyter's maw with ravage cloyed,
E'en London's ashes had been then destroyed.
Officious fear, however, to prevent
Our loss does so much more our loss augment:
The Dutch had robbed those jewels of the crown;
Our merchantmen, lest they be burned, we drown.
So when the fire did not enough devour,
The houses were demolished near the Tower.
Those ships that yearly from their teeming hole
Unloaded here the birth of either Pole
Furs from the north and silver from the west,
Wines from the south, and spices from the east;
From Gambo gold, and from the Ganges gems
Take a short voyage underneath the Thames,
Once a deep river, now with timber floored,
And shrunk, least navigable, to a ford.

Now (nothing more at Chatham left to burn),
The Holland squadron leisurely return,
And spite of Ruperts and of Albemarles,
To Ruyter's triumph lead the captive Charles.
The pleasing sight he often does prolong:
Her masts erect, tough cordage, timbers strong,
Her moving shapes, all these he does survey,
And all admires, but most his easy prey.
The seamen search her all within, without:
Viewing her strength, they yet their conquest doubt;
Then with rude shouts, secure, the air they vex,
With gamesome joy insulting on her decks.
Such the feared Hebrew, captive, blinded, shorn,
Was led about in sport, the public scorn.

Black day accursed! On thee let no man hale
Out of the port, or dare to hoist a sail,
Nor row a boat in thy unlucky hour.
Thee, the year's monster, let thy dam devour,
And constant time, to keep his course yet right,

Fill up thy space with a redoubled night.
When agèd Thames was bound with fetters base,
And Medway chaste ravished before his face,
And their dear offspring murdered in their sight,
Thou and thy fellows held'st the odious light.
Sad change since first that happy pair was wed,
When all the rivers graced their nuptial bed,
And Father Neptune promised to resign
His empire old to their immortal line!
Now with vain grief their vainer hopes they rue,
Themselves dishonoured, and the gods untrue,
And to each other, helpless couple, moan,
As the sad tortoise for the sea does groan.
But most they for their darling Charles complain,
And were it burnt, yet less would be their pain.
To see that fatal pledge of sea command
Now in the ravisher De Ruyter's hand,
The Thames roared, swooning Medway turned her tide,
And were they mortal, both for grief had died.

The court in farthing yet itself does please,
(And female Stuart there rules the four seas),
But fate does still accumulate our woes,
And Richmond her commands, as Ruyter those.

After this loss, to relish discontent,
Someone must be accused by punishment.
All our miscarriages on Pett must fall:
His name alone seems fit to answer all.
Whose counsel first did this mad war beget?
Who all commands sold through the navy? Pett.
Who would not follow when the Dutch were beat?
Who treated out the time at Bergen? Pett.
Who the Dutch fleet with storms disabled met,
And rifling prizes, them neglected? Pett.
Who with false news prevented the Gazette,
The fleet divided, writ for Rupert? Pett.
Who all our seamen cheated of their debt,
And all our prizes who did swallow? Pett.
Who did advise no navy out to set,
And who the forts left unrepairèd? Pett.
Who to supply with powder did forget
Languard, Sheerness, Gravesend and Upnor? Pett.
Who should it be but the Fanatic Pett?
Pett, the sea-architect, in making ships
Was the first cause of all these naval slips:
Had he not built, none of these faults had been;
If no creation, there had been no sin.
But his great crime, one boat away he sent,
That lost our fleet and did our flight prevent.

Then (that reward might in its turn take place,
And march with punishment in equal pace),
Southhampton dead, much of the Treasure's care
And place in council fell to Dunscombe's share.
All men admired he to that pitch could fly:
Powder ne'er blew man up so soon so high,
But sure his late good husbandry in petre
Showed him to manage the Exchequer meeter;
And who the forts would not vouchsafe a corn,
To lavish the King's money more would scorn.
Who hath no chimneys, to give all is best,
And ablest Speaker, who of law has least;
Who less estate, for Treasurer most fit,
And for a couns'llor, he that has least wit.
But the true cause was that, in's brother May,
The Exchequer might the Privy Purse obey.

But now draws near the Parliament's return;
Hyde and the court again begin to mourn:
Frequent in council, earnest in debate,
All arts they try how to prolong its date.
Grave Primate Sheldon (much in preaching there)
Blames the last session and this more does fear:
With Boynton or with Middleton 'twere sweet,
But with a Parliament abohors to meet,
And thinks 'twill ne'er be well within this nation,
Till it be governed by Convocation.
But in the Thames' mouth still De Ruyter laid;
The peace not sure, new army must be paid.
Hyde saith he hourly waits for a dispatch;
Harry came post just as he showed his watch,
All to agree the articles were clear
The Holland fleet and Parliament so near
Yet Harry must job back, and all mature,
Binding, ere the Houses meet, the treaty sure,
And 'twixt necessity and spite, till then,
Let them come up so to go down again.

Up ambles country justice on his pad,
And vest bespeaks to be more seemly clad.
Plain gentlemen in stagecoach are o'erthrown
And deputy-lieutenants in their own.
The portly burgess through the weather hot
Does for his corporation sweat and trot;
And all with sun and choler come adust
And threaten Hyde to raise a greater dust.
But fresh as from the Mint, the courtiers fine
Salute them, smiling at their vain design,
And Turner gay up to his perch does march
With face new bleached, smoothened and stiff with starch;
Tells them he at Whitehall had took a turn

And for three days thence moves them to adjourn.
`Not so!' quoth Tomkins, and straight drew his tongue,
Trusty as steel that always ready hung,
And so, proceeding in his motion warm,
The army soon raised, he doth as soon disarm.
True Trojan! While this town can girls afford,
And long as cider lasts in Herford,
The girls shall always kiss thee, though grown old,
And in eternal healths thy name be trolled.

Meanwhile the certain news of peace arrives
At court, and so reprieves their guilty lives.
Hyde orders Turner that he should come late,
Lest some new Tomkins spring a fresh debate.
The King that day raised early from his rest,
Expects (as at a play) till Turner's dressed.
At last together Ayton come and he:
No dial more could with the sun agree.
The Speaker, summoned, to the Lords repairs,
Nor gave the Commons leave to say their prayers,
But like his prisoners to the bar them led,
Where mute they stand to hear their sentence read.
Trembling with joy and fear, Hyde them prorogues,
And had almost mistook and called them rogues.

Dear Painter, draw this Speaker to the foot;
Where pencil cannot, there my pen shall do't:
That may his body, this his mind explain.
Paint him in golden gown, with mace's brain,
Bright hair, fair face, obscure and dull of head,
Like knife with ivory haft and edge of lead.
At prayers his eyes turn up the pious white,
But all the while his private bill's in sight.
In chair, he smoking sits like master cook,
And a poll bill does like his apron look.
Well was he skilled to season any question
And made a sauce, fit for Whitehall's digestion,
Whence every day, the palate more to tickle,
Court-mushrumps ready are, sent in in pickle.
When grievance urged, he swells like squatted toad,
Frisks like a frog, to croak a tax's load;
His patient piss he could hold longer than
An urinal, and sit like any hen;
At table jolly as a country host
And soaks his sack with Norfolk, like a toast;
At night, than Chanticleer more brisk and hot,
And Sergeant's wife serves him for Pertelotte.

Paint last the King, and a dead shade of night
Only dispersed by a weak taper's light,
And those bright gleams that dart along and glare

From his clear eyes, yet these too dark with care.
There, as in the calm horror all alone
He wakes, and muses of th' uneasy throne;
Raise up a sudden shape with virgin's face,
(Though ill agree her posture, hour, or place),
Naked as born, and her round arms behind
With her own tresses, interwove and twined;
Her mouth locked up, a blind before her eyes,
Yet from beneath the veil her blushes rise,
And silent tears her secret anguish speak
Her heart throbs and with very shame would break.
The object strange in him no terror moved:
He wondered first, then pitied, then he loved,
And with kind hand does the coy vision press
(Whose beauty greater seemed by her distress),
But soon shrunk back, chilled with her touch so cold,
And th' airy picture vanished from his hold.
In his deep thoughts the wonder did increase,
And he divined 'twas England or the Peace.

Express him startling next with listening ear,
As one that some unusual noise does hear.
With cannon, trumpets, drums, his door surround
But let some other painter draw the sound.
Thrice did he rise, thrice the vain tumult fled,
But again thunders, when he lies in bed.
His mind secure does the known stroke repeat
And finds the drums Louis's march did beat.

Shake then the room, and all his curtains tear
And with blue streaks infect the taper clear,
While the pale ghosts his eye does fixed admire
Of grandsire Harry and of Charles his sire.
Harry sits down, and in his open side
The grisly wound reveals of which he died,
And ghastly Charles, turning his collar low,
The purple thread about his neck does show,
Then whispering to his son in words unheard,
Through the locked door both of them disappeared.
The wondrous night the pensive King revolves,
And rising straight on Hyde's disgrace resolves.

At his first step, he Castlemaine does find,
Bennet, and Coventry, as 't were designed;
And they, not knowing, the same thing propose
Which his hid mind did in its depths enclose.
Through their feigned speech their secret hearts he knew:
To her own husband, Castlemaine untrue;
False to his master Bristol, Arlington;
And Coventry, falser than anyone,
Who to the brother, brother would betray,

Nor therefore trusts himself to such as they.
His Father's ghost, too, whispered him one note,
That who does cut his purse will cut his throat,
But in wise anger he their crimes forbears,
As thieves reprived for executioners;
While Hyde provoked, his foaming tusk does whet,
To prove them traitors and himself the Pett.

Painter, adieu! How well our arts agree,
Poetic picture, painted poetry;
But this great work is for our Monarch fit,
And henceforth Charles only to Charles shall sit.
His master-hand the ancients shall outdo,
Himself the painter and the poet too.

To the King

So his bold tube, man to the sun applied
And spots unknown to the bright star descried,
Showed they obscure him, while too near they please
And seem his courtiers, are but his disease.
Through optic trunk the planet seemed to hear,
And hurls them off e'er since in his career.

And you, Great Sir, that with him empire share,
Sun of our world, as he the Charles is there,
Blame not the Muse that brought those spots to sight,
Which in you splendour hid, corrode your light:
(Kings in the country oft have gone astray
Nor of a peasant scorned to learn the way.)
Would she the unattended throne reduce,
Banishing love, trust, ornament, and use,
Better it were to live in cloister's lock,
Or in fair fields to rule the easy flock.
She blames them only who the court restrain
And where all England serves, themselves would reign.
Bold and accursed are they that all this while
Have strove to isle our Monarch from his isle,
And to improve themselves, on false pretence,
About the Common-Prince have raised a fence;
The kingdom from the crown distinct would see
And peel the bark to burn at last the tree.
(But Ceres corn, and Flora is the spring,
Bacchus is wine, the country is the King.)

Not so does rust insinuating wear,
Nor powder so the vaulted bastion tear,
Nor earthquake so an hollow isle o'er whelm
As scratching courtiers undermine a realm,
And through the palace's foundations bore,
Burrowing themselves to hoard their guilty store.

The smallest vermin make the greatest waste,
And a poor warren once a city rased.

But they, whom born to virtue and to wealth,
Nor guilt to flattery binds, nor want to wealth,
Whose generous conscience and whose courage high
Does with clear counsels their large souls supply;
That serve the King with their estates and care,
And, as in love, on Parliaments can stare,
(Where few the number, choice is there less hard):
Give us this court, and rule without a guard.

To His Noble Friend, Mr Richard Lovelace, Upon His Poems
Sir,
Our times are much degenerate from those
Which your sweet muse with your fair fortune chose,
And as complexions alter with the climes,
Our wits have drawn the infection of our times.
That candid age no other way could tell
To be ingenious, but by speaking well.
Who best could praise had then the greatest praise,
'Twas more esteemed to give than bear the bays:
Modest ambition studied only then
To honour not herself but worthy men.
These virtues now are banished out of town,
Our Civil Wars have lost the civic crown.
He highest builds, who with most art destroys,
And against others' fame his own employs.
I see the envious caterpillar sit
On the fair blossom of each growing wit.

The air's already tainted with the swarms
Of insects which against you rise in arms:
Word-peckers, paper-rats, book-scorpions,
Of wit corrupted, the unfashioned sons.
The barbèd censurers begin to look
Like the grim consistory on thy book;
And on each line cast a reforming eye,
Severer than the young presbytery.
Till when in vain they have thee all perused,
You shall, for being faultless, be accused.
Some reading your Lucasta will allege
You wronged in her the House's privelege.
Some that you under sequestration are,
And one the book prohibits, because Kent
Their first petition by the author sent.

But when the beauteous ladies came to know
That their dear Lovelace was endangered so:

Lovelace that thawed the most congealèd breast
He who loved best and them defended best,
Whose hand so rudely grasps the steely brand,
Whose hand most gently melts the lady's hand
They all in mutiny though yet undressed
Sallied, and would in his defence contest.
And one, the loveliest that was yet e'er seen,
Thinking that I too of the rout had been,
Mine eyes invaded with a female spite,
(She knew what pain 'twould cause to lose that sight.)
`O no, mistake not,' I replied, `for I
In your defence, or in his cause, would die.'
But he, secure of glory and of time,
Above their envy, or mine aid, doth climb.
Him valiant'st men and fairest nymphs approve;
His book in them finds judgement, with you love.

Mourning
You, that decipher out the Fate
Of humane Off-springs from the Skies,
What mean these Infants which of late
Spring from the Starrs of Chlora's Eyes?

Her Eyes confus'd, and doubled ore,
With Tears suspended ere they flow;
Seem bending upwards, to restore
To Heaven, whence it came, their Woe.

When, molding of the watry Sphears,
Slow drops unty themselves away;
As if she, with those precious Tears,
Would strow the ground where Strephon lay.

Yet some affirm, pretending Art,
Her Eyes have so her Bosome drown'd,
Only to soften near her Heart
A place to fix another Wound.

And, while vain Pomp does her restrain
Within her solitary Bowr,
She courts her self in am'rous Rain;
Her self both Danae and the Showr.

Nay others, bolder, hence esteem
Joy now so much her Master grown,
That whatsoever does but seem
Like Grief, is from her Windows thrown.

Nor that she payes, while she survives,

To her dead Love this Tribute due;
But casts abroad these Donatives,
At the installing of a new.

How wide they dream! The Indian Slaves
That sink for Pearl through Seas profound,
Would find her Tears yet deeper Waves
And not of one the bottom sound.

I yet my silent Judgment keep,
Disputing not what they believe:
But sure as oft as Women weep,
It is to be suppos'd they grieve.

A Poem On The Statue At Stocks–Market.
As cities that to the fierce conqueror yield,
Do at their own charges their cittadals build;
So Sir Robert advanc'd the King's statue, in token
Of bankers defeated and Lombard-street broken.
Some thought it a knightly and generous deed,
Obliging the citty with a King and a steed
When with honour he might from his word have gone back:
He that vows for a calme, is absolved by a wreck.
But now it appears, from the first to the last.
To be all a revenge, and a malice forecast;
Upon the King's birth-day to set up a thing.
That shows him a monkey more like than a King.
When each one that passes finds fault with the horse,
Yet all do affirme that the King is much worse;
And some by the likeness Sir Robert suspect.
That he did for the King his own statue erect.
Thus to see him disfigur'd — the herb-women chide,
Who up on their panniers more gracefully ride;
And so loose in his seat — that all persons agree,
Ev'n Sir Willuan Peake sits much firmer than he.
But a market, as some say, doth fit the King well,
Who the Parliament too — and revenue doth sell;
And others, to make the similitude hold.
Say his Majesty too — is oft purchased and sold.
This statue is sorely more scandalous far
Than all the Dutch pictures which caused the Warr;
And what the exchequer for that took on trust
May we henceforth confiscate, for reasons more just.
But Sir Robert, to take all the scandal away.
Does the errour upon the artificer lay;
And alledges the workmanship was not his own,
For he counterfeits only in gold — not in stone.
But, Sir Knight of the Vine, how came't in your thought.
That when to the scaffold your liege you had brought,

With canvass and deales you e'er since do him cloud,
As if you had meant it his coffin and shrowdt
Hath Blood [stole] him away, as his crown he convey'd?
Or is he to Clayton's gone in masquerade
Or is he in caball in his cabinett sett
Or have you to the Compter remov'd him for debt?
Methinks by the equipage of this vile scene.
That to change him into a Jack-pudding you mean;
Or why thus expose him to popular flouts.
As if we'd as good have a King made of Clouts
Or do you his faults out of modesty vaile
With three shattered planks, and the rag of a saile;
To express how his navy was shattered and torn.
The day that he was both restored and born?
Sure the King will ne'er think of repaying his bankers.
When loyalty now — all expires with his spankers;
If the Indies and Smyrna do not him enrich,
He will hardly have left a poor ragg to his breech.
But Sir Robert affirmes that we do him much wrong,
'Tis the 'Graver at work, to reform him — so long:
But, alas! he will never arrive at his end,
For it is such a King as no chissel can mend.
But with all his errours — restore us our King,
If ever you hope in December — for Spring;
For though all the world cannot show such another,
Yet we'd better have him than his bigotted brother.

On A Drop Of Dew
See how the Orient Dew,
Shed from the Bosom of the Morn
Into the blowing Roses,
Yet careless of its Mansion new;
For the clear Region where 'twas born
Round in its self incloses:
And in its little Globes Extent,
Frames as it can its native Element.
How it the purple flow'r does slight,
Scarce touching where it lyes,
But gazing back upon the Skies,
Shines with a mournful Light;
Like its own Tear,
Because so long divided from the Sphear.
Restless it roules and unsecure,
Trembling lest it grow impure:
Till the warm Sun pitty it's Pain,
And to the Skies exhale it back again.
So the Soul, that Drop, that Ray
Of the clear Fountain of Eternal Day,
Could it within the humane flow'r be seen,

Remembring still its former height,
Shuns the sweat leaves and blossoms green;
And, recollecting its own Light,
Does, in its pure and circling thoughts, express
The greater Heaven in an Heaven less.
In how coy a Figure wound,
Every way it turns away:
So the World excluding round,
Yet receiving in the Day.
Dark beneath, but bright above:
Here disdaining, there in Love.
How loose and easie hence to go:
How girt and ready to ascend.
Moving but on a point below,
It all about does upwards bend.
Such did the Manna's sacred Dew destil;
White, and intire, though congeal'd and chill.
Congeal'd on Earth: but does, dissolving, run
Into the Glories of th' Almighty Sun.

The Character Of Holland
Holland, that scarce deserves the name of Land,
As but th'Off-scouring of the Brittish Sand;
And so much Earth as was contributed
By English Pilots when they heav'd the Lead;
Or what by th' Oceans slow alluvion fell,
Of shipwrackt Cockle and the Muscle-shell;
This indigested vomit of the Sea
Fell to the Dutch by just Propriety.
Glad then, as Miners that have found the Oar,
They with mad labour fish'd the Land to Shoar;
And div'd as desperately for each piece
Of Earth, as if't had been of Ambergreece;
Collecting anxiously small Loads of Clay,
Less then what building Swallows bear away;
Transfursing into them their Dunghil Soul.
How did they rivet, with Gigantick Piles,
Thorough the Center their new-catched Miles;
And to the stake a strugling Country bound,
Where barking Waves still bait the forced Ground;
Building their watry Babel far more high
To reach the Sea, then those to scale the Sky.
Yet still his claim the Injur'd Ocean laid,
And oft at Leap-frog ore their Steeples plaid:
As if on purpose it on Land had come
To shew them what's their Mare Liberum.
A daily deluge over them does boyl;
The Earth and Water play at Level-coyl;
The Fish oft-times the Burger dispossest,

And sat not as a Meat but as a Guest;
And oft the Tritons and the Sea-Nymphs saw
Whole sholes of Dutch serv'd up for Cabillan;
Or as they over the new Level rang'd
For pickled Herring, pickled Heeren chang'd.
Nature, it seem'd, asham'd of her mistake,
Would throw their land away at Duck and Drake.
Therefore Necessity, that first made Kings,
Something like Government among them brings.
For as with Pygmees who best kills the Crane,
Among the hungry he that treasures Grain,
Among the blind the one-ey'd blinkard reigns,
So rules among the drowned he that draines.
Not who first see the rising Sun commands,
But who could first discern the rising Lands.
Who best could know to pump an Earth so leak
Him they their Lord and Country's Father speak.
To make a Bank was a great Plot of State;
Invent a Shov'l and be a Magistrate.
Hence some small Dyke-grave unperceiv'd invades
The Pow'r, and grows as 'twere a King of Spades.
But for less envy some Joynt States endures,
Who look like a Commission of the Sewers.
For these Half-anders, half wet, and half dry,
Nor bear strict service, nor pure Liberty.
'Tis probable Religion after this
Came next in order; which they could not miss.
How could the Dutch but be converted, when
Th' Apostles were so many Fishermen?
Besides the Waters of themselves did rise,
And, as their Land, so them did re-baptise.
Though Herring for their God few voices mist,
And Poor-John to have been th' Evangelist.
Faith, that could never Twins conceive before,
Never so fertile, spawn'd upon this shore:
More pregnant then their Marg'ret, that laid down
For Hans-in-Kelder of a whole Hans-Town.
Sure when Religion did it self imbark,
And from the east would Westward steer its Ark,
It struck, and splitting on this unknown ground,
Each one thence pillag'd the first piece he found:
Hence Amsterdam, Turk-Christian-Pagan-Jew,
Staple of Sects and Mint of Schisme grew;
That Bank of Conscience, where not one so strange
Opinion but finds Credit, and Exchange.
In vain for Catholicks our selves we bear;
The Universal Church is onely there.
Nor can Civility there want for Tillage,
Where wisely for their Court they chose a Village.
How fit a Title clothes their Governours,
Themselves the Hogs as all their Subjects Bores

Let it suffice to give their Country Fame
That it had one Civilis call'd by Name,
Some Fifteen hundred and more years ago,
But surely never any that was so.
See but their Mairmaids with their Tails of Fish,
Reeking at Church over the Chafing-Dish.
A vestal Turf enshrin'd in Earthen Ware
Fumes through the loop-holes of wooden Square.
Each to the Temple with these Altars tend,
But still does place it at her Western End:
While the fat steam of Female Sacrifice
Fills the Priests Nostrils and puts out his Eyes.
Or what a Spectacle the Skipper gross,
A Water-Hercules Butter-Coloss,
Tunn'd up with all their sev'ral Towns of Beer;
When Stagg'ring upon some Land, Snick and Sneer,
They try, like Statuaries, if they can,
Cut out each others Athos to a Man:
And carve in their large Bodies, where they please,
The Armes of the United Provinces.
But when such Amity at home is show'd;
What then are their confederacies abroad?
Let this one court'sie witness all the rest;
When their hole Navy they together prest,
Not Christian Captives to redeem from Bands:
Or intercept the Western golden Sands:
No, but all ancient Rights and Leagues must vail,
Rather then to the English strike their sail;
to whom their weather-beaten Province ows
It self, when as some greater Vessal tows
A Cock-boat tost with the same wind and fate;
We buoy'd so often up their Sinking State.
Was this Jus Belli & Pacis; could this be
Cause why their Burgomaster of the Sea
Ram'd with Gun-powder, flaming with Brand wine,
Should raging hold his Linstock to the Mine?
While, with feign'd Treaties, they invade by stealth
Our sore new circumcised Common wealth.
Yet of his vain Attempt no more he sees
Then of Case-Butter shot and Bullet-Cheese.
And the torn Navy stagger'd with him home,
While the Sea laught it self into a foam,
'Tis true since that (as fortune kindly sports,)
A wholesome Danger drove us to our ports.
While half their banish'd keels the Tempest tost,
Half bound at home in Prison to the frost:
That ours mean time at leisure might careen,
In a calm Winter, under Skies Serene.
As the obsequious Air and waters rest,
Till the dear Halcyon hatch out all its nest.
The Common wealth doth by its losses grow;

And, like its own Seas, only Ebbs to flow.
Besides that very Agitation laves,
And purges out the corruptible waves.
And now again our armed Bucentore
Doth yearly their Sea-Nuptials restore.
And how the Hydra of seaven Provinces
Is strangled by our Infant Hercules.
Their Tortoise wants its vainly stretched neck;
Their Navy all our Conquest or our Wreck:
Or, what is left, their Carthage overcome
Would render fain unto our better Rome.
Unless our Senate, lest their Youth disuse,
The War, (but who would) Peace if begg'd refuse.
For now of nothing may our State despair,
Darling of Heaven, and of Men the Care;
Provided that they be what they have been,
Watchful abroad, and honest still within.
For while our Neptune doth a Trident shake, Blake,
Steel'd with those piercing Heads, Dean, Monck and
And while Jove governs in the highest Sphere,
Vainly in Hell let Pluto domineer.

The Loyal Scot.
By Cleveland's Ghost, upon the death of Captain Douglas, burned on his ship at Chatham.

Of the old heroes when the warlike shades
Saw Douglas marching on the Elysian glades.
They all, consulting, gathered in a ring,
Which of their poets should his welcome sing;
And, as a favourable penance, chose
Cleveland, on whom they would that task impose.
He understood, but willingly addressed
His ready muse, to court that noble guest.
Much had he cured the tumour of his vein,
He judged more clearly now and saw more plain;
For those soft airs had tempered every thought,
Since of wise Lethe he had drunk a draught.
Abruptly he begun, disguising art.
As of his satire this had been a part.
As so, brave Douglas, on whose lovely chin
The early down but newly did begin.
And modest beauty yet his sex did veil,
While envious virgins hope he is a male,
His yellow locks curl back themselves to seek,
Nor other courtship know but to his cheek.
Oft as he in chill Esk or Tyne, by night,
Hardened and cooled his limbs, so soft, so white,
Among the reeds, to be espied by him,
The nymphs would rustle, he would forward swim.

They sighed, and said, Fond boy, why so untame,
That fly'st love's fires, reserved for other flame?
First on his ship he faced that horrid day.
And wondered much at those that ran away.
No other fear himself could comprehend.
Than lest Heaven fall ere thither he ascend:
But entertains the while his time, too short.
With birding at the Dutch, as if in sport;
Or waves his sword, and, could he them conjure
"Within his circle, knows himself secure.
The fatal bark him boards with grappling fire,
And safely through its port the Dutch retire.
That precious life he yet disdains to save,
Or with known art to try the gentle wave.
Much him the honour of his ancient race
Inspired, nor would he his own deeds deface;
And secret joy in his calm soul does rise.
That Monck looks on to see how Douglas dies.
Like a glad lover the fierce flames he meets.
And tries his first embraces in their sheets;
His shape exact, which the bright flames enfold,
Like the sun's statue stands of burnished gold;
Round the transparent fire about him glows,
As the clear amber on the bee docs close;
And, as on angels' heads their glories shine,
His burning locks adorn his face divine.
But when in his immortal mind he felt
His altering form and soldered limbs to melt,
Down on the deck he laid himself, and died,
With his dear sword reposing by his side.
And on the flaming plank so rests his head.
As one that warmed himself, and went to bed.
His ship bums down, and with his relics sinks.
And the sad stream beneath his ashes drinks.
Fortunate boy! if either pencil's fame,
Or if my verse can propagate thy name,
When CEta and Alcides are forgot,
Our English youth shall sing the valiant Scot.
Skip saddles, Pegasus, thou needst not brag.
Sometimes the Galloway proves the better nag.
Shall not a death so generous, when told,
Unite our distance, fill our breaches old?
So in the Roman forum, Curtius brave,
Galloping down, closed up the gaping cave.
No more discourse of Scotch and English race,
Nor chant the fabulous hunt of Chevy-Chase;
Mixed in Corinthian metal at thy flame.
Our nations melting, thy Colossus frame.
Prick down the point, whoever has the art.
Where nature Scotland does from England part;
Anatomists may sooner fix the cells

Where life resides and understanding dwells.
But this we know, though that exceeds our skill,
That whosoever separates them does ill.
Will you the Tweed that sullen bounder call.
Of soil, of wit, of manners, and of all?
Why draw you not, as well, the thrifty line
From Thames, Trent, Humber, or at least the Tyne?
So may we the state-corpulence redress.
And little England, when we please, make less.
What ethic river is this wondrous Tweed,
Whose one bank virtue, t'other vice, does breed?
Or what new perpendicular does rise
Up from her streams, continued to the skies,
That between us the common air should bar.
And split the influence of every star?
But who considers right, will find indeed,
'Tis Holy Island parts us, not the Tweed.
Nothing but clergy could us two seclude,
No Scotch was ever like a bishop's feud.
All Litanies in this have wanted faith,
There's no deliver us from a bishop's wrath
Never shall Calvin pardoned be for Sales,
Never, for Burnet's sake, the Lauderdales;
For Becket's sake, Kent always shall have tails.
Who sermons e'er can pacify and prayers?
Or to the joint stools reconcile the chairs?
Though kingdoms join, yet church will kirk oppose;
The mitre still divides, the crown does close;
As in Rogation week they whip us round,
To keep in mind the Scotch and English bound.
What the ocean binds is by the bishops rent,
Then seas make islands in our continent.
Nature in vain us in one land compiles,
If the cathedral still shall have its isles.
Nothing, not bogs nor sands nor seas nor Alps,
Separates the world so as the bishops' scalps;
Stretch for the line their surcingle alone,
'Twill make a more unhabitable zone.
The friendly loadstone has not more combined.
Than bishops cramped the commerce of mankind.
Had it not been for such a bias strong.
Two nations ne'er had missed the mark so long.
The world in all doth but two nations bear.
The good, the bad, and these mixed everywhere;
Under each pole place either of these two,
The bad will basely, good will bravely, do;
And few, indeed, can parallel our climes,
For worth heroic, or heroic crimes.
The trial would, however, be too nice.
Which stronger were, a Scotch or English vice;
Or whether the same virtue would reflect,

From Scotch or English heart, the same effect.
Nation is all, but name, a Shibboleth,
Where a mistaken accent causes death.
In Paradise names only nature showed,
At Babel names from pride and discord flowed;
And ever since men, with a female spite.
First call each other names, and then they fight.
Scotland and England cause of just uproar;
Do man and wife signify rogue and whore?
Say but a Scot and straight we fall to sides;
That syllable like a Picts' wall divides.
Rational men's words pledges are of peace;
Perverted, serve dissension to increase.
For shame! extirpate from each loyal breast
That senseless rancour, against interest.
One king, one faith, one language, and one isle,
English and Scotch, 'tis all but cross and pile.
Charles, our great soul J this only understands;
He our affections both, and wills, commands;
And where twin-sympathies cannot atone,
Knows the last secret, how to make us one.
Just so the prudent husbandman, that sees
The idle tumult of his factious bees,
The morning dews, and flowers, neglected grown,
The hive a comb-case, every bee a drone,
Powders them o'er, till none discerns his foes.
And all themselves in meal and friendship lose;
The insect kingdom straight begins to thrive.
And all work honey for the common hive.
Pardon, young hero, this so long transport,
Thy death more noble did the same extort.
My former satire for this verse forget,
My fault against my recantation set.
I single did against a nation write,
Against a nation thou didst singly fight.
My differing crimes do more thy virtue raise,
And, such my rashness, best thy valour praise.
Here Douglas smiling said, he did intend,
After such frankness shown, to be his friend;
Forewarned him therefore, lest in time he were
Metempsychosed to some Scotch Presbyter.

Music's Empire
First was the world as one great cymbal made,
Where jarring winds to infant Nature played.
All music was a solitary sound,
To hollow rocks and murm'ring fountains bound.

Jubal first made the wilder notes agree;

And Jubal tuned music's Jubilee;
He call'd the echoes from their sullen cell,
And built the organ's city where they dwell.

Each sought a consort in that lovely place,
And virgin trebles wed the manly bass.
From whence the progeny of numbers new
Into harmonious colonies withdrew.

Some to the lute, some to the viol went,
And others chose the cornet eloquent,
These practicing the wind, and those the wire,
To sing men's triumphs, or in Heaven's choir.

Then music, the mosaic of the air,
Did of all these a solemn noise prepare;
With which she gain'd the empire of the ear,
Including all between the earth and sphere.

Victorious sounds! yet here your homage do
Unto a gentler conqueror than you;
Who though he flies the music of his praise,
Would with you Heaven's Hallelujahs raise.

On Mr Milton's Paradise Lost
When I beheld the Poet blind, yet bold,
In slender Book his vast Design unfold,
Messiah Crown'd, Gods Reconcil'd Decree,
Rebelling Angels, the Forbidden Tree,
Heav'n, Hell, Earth, Chaos, All; the Argument
Held me a while misdoubting his Intent,
That he would ruine (for I saw him strong)
The sacred Truths to Fable and old Song,
(So Sampson groap'd the Temples Posts in spight)
The World o'rewhelming to revenge his Sight.
Yet as I read, soon growing less severe,
I lik'd his Project, the success did fear;
Through that wide Field how he his way should find
O're which lame Faith leads Understanding blind;
Lest he perplext the things he would explain,
And what was easie he should render vain.
Or if a Work so infinite he spann'd,
Jealous I was that some less skilful hand
(Such as disquiet alwayes what is well,
And by ill imitating would excell)
Might hence presume the whole Creations day
To change in Scenes, and show it in a Play.
Pardon me, Mighty Poet, nor despise
My causeless, yet not impious, surmise.

But I am now convinc'd, and none will dare
Within thy Labours to pretend a Share.
Thou hast not miss'd one thought that could be fit,
And all that was improper dost omit:
So that no room is here for Writers left,
But to detect their Ignorance or Theft.
That Majesty which through thy Work doth Reign
Draws the Devout, deterring the Profane.
And things divine thou treats of in such state
As them preserves, and Thee in violate.
At once delight and horrour on us seize,
Thou singst with so much gravity and ease;
And above humane flight dost soar aloft,
With Plume so strong, so equal, and so soft.
The Bird nam'd from that Paradise you sing
So never Flags, but alwaies keeps on Wing.
Where couldst thou Words of such a compass find?
Whence furnish such a vast expense of Mind?
Just Heav'n Thee, like Tiresias, to requite,
Rewards with Prophesie thy loss of Sight.
Well might thou scorn thy Readers to allure
With tinkling Rhime, of thy own Sense secure;
While the Town-Bays writes all the while and spells,
And like a Pack-Horse tires without his Bells.
Their Fancies like our bushy Points appear,
The Poets tag them; we for fashion wear.
I too transported by the Mode offend,
And while I meant to Praise thee, must Commend.
Thy verse created like thy Theme sublime,
In Number, Weight, and Measure, needs not Rhime.

The Coronet
When for the Thorns with which I long, too long,
With many a piercing wound,
My Saviours head have crown'd,
I seek with Garlands to redress that Wrong:
Through every Garden, every Mead,
I gather flow'rs (my fruits are only flow'rs)
Dismantling all the fragrant Towers
That once adorn'd my Shepherdesses head.
And now when I have summ'd up all my store,
Thinking (so I my self deceive)
So rich a Chaplet thence to weave
As never yet the king of Glory wore:
Alas I find the Serpent old
That, twining in his speckled breast,
About the flow'rs disguis'd does fold,
With wreaths of Fame and Interest.
Ah, foolish Man, that would'st debase with them,

And mortal Glory, Heavens Diadem!
But thou who only could'st the Serpent tame,
Either his slipp'ry knots at once untie,
And disintangle all his winding Snare:
Or shatter too with him my curious frame:
And let these wither, so that he may die,
Though set with Skill and chosen out with Care.
That they, while Thou on both their Spoils dost tread,
May crown thy Feet, that could not crown thy Head.

A Poem Upon The Death Of His Late Highness The Lord Protector
That Providence which had so long the care
Of Cromwell's head, and numbered every hair,
Now in itself (the glass where all appears)
Had seen the period of his golden years:
And thenceforh only did attend to trace
What death might least so fair a life deface.

The people, which what most they fear esteem,
Death when more horrid, so more noble deem,
And blame the last act, like spectators vain,
Unless the prince whom they applaud be slain.
Nor fate indeed can well refuse that right
To those that lived in war, to die in fight.

But long his valour none had left that could
Endanger him, or clemency that would.
And he whom Nature all for peace had made,
But angry heaven unto war had swayed,
And so less useful where he most desired,
For what he least affected was admired,
Deservèd yet an end whose every part,
Should speak the wondrous softness of his heart.

To Love and Grief the fatal writ was 'signed;
(Those nobler weaknesses of human kind,
From which those powers that issued the decree,
Although immortal, found they were not free),
That they, to whom his breast still open lies,
In gentle passions should his death disguise:
And leave succeeding ages cause to mourn,
As long as Grief shall weep, or Love shall burn.

Straight does a slow and languishing disease
Eliza, Nature's and his darling, seize.
Her when an infant, taken with her charms,
He oft would flourish in his mighty arms,
And, lest their force the tender burden wrong,
Slacken the vigour of his muscles strong;

Then to the Mother's breast her softly move,
Which while she drained of milk, she filled with love.
But as with riper years her virtue grew,
And every minute adds a lustre new,
When with meridian height her beauty shined,
And thorough that sparkled her fairer mind,
When she with smiles serene in words discreet
His hidden soul at ever turn could meet;
Then might y'ha' daily his affection spied,
Doubling that knot which destiny had tied,
While they by sense, not knowing, comprehend
How on each other both their fates depend.
With her each day the pleasing hours he shares,
And at her aspect calms his growing cares;
Or with a grandsire's joy her children sees
Hanging about her neck or at his knees.
Hold fast, dear infants, hold them both or none;
This will not stay when once the other's gone.

A silent fire now wastes those limbs of wax,
And him within his tortured image racks.
So the flower withering which the garden crowned,
The sad root pines in secret under ground.
Each groan he doubled and each sigh he sighed,
Repeated over to the restless night.
No trembling string composed to numbers new,
Answers the touch in notes more sad, more true.
She, lest he grieve, hides what she can her pains,
And he to lessen hers his sorrow feigns:
Yet both perceived, yet both concealed their skills,
And so diminishing increased their ills:
That whether by each other's grief they fell,
Or on their own redoubled, none can tell.

And now Eliza's purple locks were shorn,
Where she so long her Father's fate had worn:
And frequent lightning to her soul that flies,
Divides the air, and opens all the skies:
And now his life, suspended by her breath,
Ran out impetuously to hasting death.
Like polished mirrors, so his steely breast
Had every figure of her woes expressed,
And with the damp of her last gasp obscured,
Had drawn such stains as were not to be cured.
Fate could not either reach with single stroke,
But the dear image fled, the mirror broke.

Who now shall tell us more of mournful swans,
Of halcyons kind, or bleeding pelicans?
No downy breast did e'er so gently beat,
Or fan with airy plumes so soft an heat.

For he no duty by his height excused,
Nor, though a prince, to be a man refused:
But rather than in his Eliza's pain
Not love, not grieve, would neither live nor reign:
And in himself so oft immortal tried,
Yet in compassion of another died.

So have I seen a vine, whose lasting age
Of many a winter hath survived the rage,
Under whose shady tent men every year
At its rich blood's expense their sorrow cheer,
If some dear branch where it extends its life
Chance to be pruned by an untimely knife,
The parent-tree unto the grief succeeds,
And through the wound its vital humour bleeds,
Trickling in watery drops, whose flowing shape
Weeps that it falls ere fixed into a grape.
So the dry stock, no more that spreading vine,
Frustrates the autumn and the hopes of wine.

A secret cause does sure those signs ordain
Foreboding princes' falls, and seldom vain.
Whether some kinder powers that wish us well,
What they above cannot prevent foretell;
Or the great world do by consent presage,
As hollow seas with future tempests rage;
Or rather heaven, which us so long foresees,
Their funerals celebrates while it decrees.
But never yet was any human fate
By Nature solemnized with so much state.
He unconcerned the dreadful passage crossed;
But, oh, what pangs that death did Nature cost!

First the great thunder was shot off, and sent
The signal from the starry battlement.
The winds receive it, and its force outdo,
As practising how they could thunder too;
Out of the binder's hand the sheaves they tore,
And thrashed the harvest in the airy floor;
Or of huge trees, whose growth with his did rise,
The deep foundations opened to the skies.
Then heavy show'rs the wingèd tempests lead,
And pour the deluge o'er the chaos' head.
The race of warlike horses at his tomb
Offer themselves in many a hecatomb;
With pensive head towards the ground they fall,
And helpless languish at the tainted stall.
Numbers of men decrease with pains unknown,
And hasten, not to see his death, their own.
Such tortures all the elements unfixed,
Troubled to part where so exactly mixed.

And as through air his wasting spirits flowed,
The universe laboured beneath their load.

Nature, it seemed with him would Nature vie;
He with Eliza. It with him would die,
He without noise still travelled to his end,
As silent suns to meet the night descend.
The stars that for him fought had only power
Left to determine now his final hour,
Which, since they might not hinder, yet they cast
To choose it worthy of his glories past.

No part of time but bare his mark away
Of honour; all the year was Cromwell's day:
But this, of all the most ausicious found,
Twice had in open field him victor crowned:
When up the armèd mountains of Dunbar
He marched, and through deep Severn ending war.
What day should him eternize but the same
That had before immortalized his name?
That so who ere would at his death have joyed,
In their own griefs might find themselves employed;
But those that sadly his departure grieved,
Yet joyed, remebering what he once achieved.
And the last minute his victorious ghost
Gave chase to Ligny on the Belgic coast.
Here ended all his mortal toils: he laid
And slept in place under the laurel shade.

O Cromwell, Heaven's Favourite! To none
Have such high honours from above been shown:
For whom the elements we mourners see,
And heaven itself would the great herald be,
Which with more care set forth his obsequies
Than those of Moses hid from human eyes,
As jealous only here lest all be less,
That we could to his memory express.
Then let us to our course of mourning keep:
Where heaven leads, 'tis piety to weep.
Stand back, ye seas, and shrunk beneath the veil
Of your abyss, with covered head bewail
Your Monarch: we demand not your supplies
To compass in our isle; our tears suffice:
Since him away the dismal tempest rent,
Who once more joined us to the continent;
Who planted England on the Flandric shore,
And stretched our frontier to the Indian ore;
Whose greater truths obscure the fables old,
Whether of British saints or Worthies told;
And in a valour lessening Arthur's deeds,
For holiness the Confessor exceeds.

He first put arms into Religion's hand,
And timorous Conscience unto Courage manned:
The soldier taught that inward mail to wear,
And fearing God how they should nothing fear.
`Those strokes,' he said, `will pierce through all below
Where those that strike from heaven fetch their blow.'
Astonished armies did their flight prepare,
And cities strong were stormèd by his prayer;
Of that, forever Preston's field shall tell
The story, and impregnable Clonmel.
And where the sandy mountain Fenwick scaled,
The sea between, yet hence his prayer prevailed.
What man was ever so in heaven obeyed
Since the commanded sun o'er Gideon stayed?
In all his wars needs must he triumph when
He conquered God still ere he fought with men:

Hence, though in battle none so brave or fierce,
Yet him the adverse steel could never pierce.
Pity it seemed to hurt him more that felt
Each wound himself which he to others dealt;
Danger itself refusing to offend
So loose an enemy, so fast a friend.

Friendship, that sacred virtue, long does claim
The first foundation of his house and name:
But within one its narrow limits fall,
His tenderness extended unto all.
And that deep soul through every channel flows,
Where kindly nature loves itself to lose.
More strong affections never reason served,
Yet still affected most what best deserved.
If he Eliza loved to that degree,
(Though who more worthy to be loved than she?)
If so indulgent to his own, how dear
To him the children of the highest were?
For her he once did nature's tribute pay:
For these his life adventured every day:
And 'twould be found, could we his thoughts have cast,
Their griefs struck deepest, if Eliza's last.

What prudence more than human did he need
To keep so dear, so differing minds agreed?
The worser sort, as conscious of their ill,
Lie weak and easy to the ruler's will;
But to the good (too many or too few)
All law is useless, all reward is due.
Oh ill-advised, if not for love, for shame,
Spare yet your own, if you neglect his fame;
Lest others dare to think your zeal a mask,

And you to govern, only heaven's task.

Valour, religion, friendship, prudence died
At once with him, and all that's good beside;
And we death's refuse, nature's dregs, confined
To loathsome life, alas! are left behind.
Where we (so once we used) shall now no more
To fetch the day, press about his chamber door
From which he issued with that awful state,
It seemd Mars broke through Janus' double gate,
Yet always tempered with an air so mild,
No April suns that e'er so gently smiled
No more shall hear that powerful language charm,
Whose force oft spared the labour of his arm:
No more shall follow where he spent the days
In war, in counsel, or in prayer and praise,
Whose meanest acts he would himself advance,
As ungirt David to the ark did dance.
All, all is gone of our or his delight
In horses fierce, wild deer, or armour bright;
Francisca fair can nothing now but weep,
Nor with soft notes shall sing his cares asleep.

I saw him dead. A leaden slumber lies
And mortal sleep over those wakeful eyes:
Those gentle rays under the lids were fled,
Which through his looks that piercing sweetness shed;
That port which so majestic was and strong,
Loose and deprived of vigour, stretched along:
All withered, all discoloured, pale and wan
How much another thing, nor more that man?
Oh human glory vain, oh death, oh wings,
Oh worthless world, oh transitory things!

Yet dwelt that greatnesss in his shape decayed,
That still through dead, greater than death he laid:
And in his altered face you something feign
That threatens death he yet will live again.

Not much unlike the sacred oak which shoots
To heaven its branches and through earth its roots,
Whose spacious bought are hung with trophies round,
And honoured wreaths have oft the victor crowned.
When angry Jove darts lightning through the air,
At mortals' sins, nor his own plant will spare,
(It groans, and bruises all below, that stood
So many years the shelter of the wood.)
The tree erewhile foreshortened to our view,
When fall'n shows taller yet than as it grew:

So shall his praise to after times increase,

When truth shall be allowed, and faction cease,
And his own shadows with him fall. The eye
Detracts from object than itself more high:
But when death takes them from that envied seat,
Seeing how little, we confess how great.

Thee, many ages hence in martial verse
Shall the English soldier, ere he charge, rehearse,
Singing of thee, inflame themselves to fight,
And with the name of Cromwell, armies fright.
As long as rivers to the seas shall run,
As long as Cynthia shall relieve the sun,
While stags shall fly unto the firests thick,
While sheep delight the grassy downs to pick,
As long as future times succeeds the past,
Always they honour, praise, and name shall last.

Thou in a pitch how far beyond the sphere
Of human glory tower'st, and reigning there
Despoiled of mortal robes, in seas of bliss,
Plunging dost bathe, and tread the bright abyss:
There thy great soul yet once a world does see,
Spacious enough, and pure enough for thee.
How soon thou Moses hast, and Joshua found,
And David for the sword and harp renowned?
How straight canst to each happy mansion go?
(Far better known above than here below)
And in those joys dost spend the endless day,
Which in expressing we ourselves betray.

For we, since thou art gone, with heavy doom,
Wander like ghosts about thy lovèd tomb;
And lost in tears, have neither sight nor mind
To guide us upward through this region blind.
Since thou art gone, who best that way couldst teach,
Only our sighs, perhaps, may thither reach.

And Richard yet, where his great parent led,
Beats on the rugged track: he, virtue dead,
Revives, and by his milder beams assures;
And yet how much of them his grief obscures?

He, as his father, long was kept from sight
In private, to be viewed by better light;
But opened once, what splendour does he throw?
A Cromwell in an hour a prince will grow.
How he becomes that seat, how strongly strains,
How gently winds at once the ruling reins?
Heaven to this choice prepared a diadem,
Richer than any Easter silk or gem;
A pearly rainbow, where the sun enchased

His brows, like an imperial jewel graced.

We find already what those omens mean,
Earth ne'er more glad, nor heaven more serene.
Cease now our griefs, calm peace succeeds a war,
Rainbows to storms, Richard to Oliver.
Tempt not his clemency to try his power,
He threats no deluge, yet foretells a shower.

The Definition Of Love
My Love is of a birth as rare
As 'tis for object strange and high:
It was begotten by despair
Upon Impossibility.

Magnanimous Despair alone.
Could show me so divine a thing,
Where feeble Hope could ne'r have flown
But vainly flapt its Tinsel Wing.

And yet I quickly might arrive
Where my extended Soul is fixt,
But Fate does Iron wedges drive,
And alwaies crouds it self betwixt.

For Fate with jealous Eye does see.
Two perfect Loves; nor lets them close:
Their union would her ruine be,
And her Tyrannick pow'r depose.

And therefore her Decrees of Steel
Us as the distant Poles have plac'd,
(Though Loves whole World on us doth wheel)
Not by themselves to be embrac'd.

Unless the giddy Heaven fall,
And Earth some new Convulsion tear;
And, us to joyn, the World should all
Be cramp'd into a Planisphere.

As Lines so Loves Oblique may well
Themselves in every Angle greet:
But ours so truly Paralel,
Though infinite can never meet.

Therefore the Love which us doth bind,
But Fate so enviously debarrs,
Is the Conjunction of the Mind,
And Opposition of the Stars.

Fleckno, An English Priest At Rome
Oblig'd by frequent visits of this man,
Whom as Priest, Poet, and Musician,
I for some branch of Melchizedeck took,
(Though he derives himself from my Lord Brooke)
I sought his Lodging; which is at the Sign
Of the sad Pelican; Subject divine
For Poetry: There three Stair Cases high,
Which signifies his triple property,
I found at last a Chamber, as 'twas said,
But seem'd a Coffin set on the Stairs head.
Not higher then Seav'n, nor larger then three feet;
Only there was nor Seeling, nor a Sheet,
Save that th' ingenious Door did as you come
Turn in, and shew to Wainscot half the Room.
Yet of his State no man could have complain'd;
There being no Bed where he entertain'd:
And though within one Cell so narrow pent,
He'd Stanza's for a whole Appartement.
Straight without further information,
In hideous verse, he, and a dismal tone,
Begins to exercise; as if I were
Possest; and sure the Devil brought me there.
But I, who now imagin'd my selfbrought
To my last Tryal, in a serious thought
Calm'd the disorders of my youthful Breast,
And to my Martyrdom prepared Rest.
Only this frail Ambition did remain,
The last distemper of the sober Brain,
That there had been some present to assure
The future Ages how I did indure:
And how I, silent, turn'd my burning Ear
Towards the Verse; and when that could n
Held him the other; and unchanged yet,
Ask'd still for more, and pray'd him to repeat:
Till the Tyrant, weary to persecute,
Left off, and try'd t'allure me with his Lute.
Now as two Instruments, to the same key
Being tun'd by Art, if the one touched be
The other opposite as soon replies,
Mov'd by the Air and hidden Sympathies;
So while he with his gouty Fingers craules
Over the Lute, his murmuring Belly calls,
Whose hungry Guts to the same streightness twin'd
In Echo to the trembling Strings repin'd.
I, that perceiv'd now what his Musick ment,
Ask'd civilly if he had eat this Lent.
He answered yes; with such, and such an one.

For he has this of gen'rous, that alone
He never feeds; save only when he tryes
With gristly Tongue to dart the passing Flyes.
I ask'd if he eat flesh. And he, that was
So hungry that though ready to say Mass
Would break his fast before, said he was Sick,
And th' Ordinance was only Politick.
Nor was I longer to invite him: Scant
Happy at once to make him Protestant,
And Silent. Nothing now Dinner stay'd
But till he had himself a Body made.
I mean till he were drest: for else so thin
He stands, as if he only fed had been
With consecrated Wafers: and the Host
Hath sure more flesh and blood then he can boast.
This Basso Relievo of a Man,
Who as a Camel tall, yet easly can
The Needles Eye thread without any stich,
(His only impossible is to be rich)
Lest his too suttle Body, growing rare,
Should leave his Soul to wander in the Air,
He therefore circumscribes himself in rimes;
And swaddled in's own papers seaven times,
Wears a close Jacket of poetick Buff,
With which he doth his third Dimension Stuff.
Thus armed underneath, he over all
Does make a primitive Sotana fall;
And above that yet casts an antick Cloak,
Worn at the first Counsel of Antioch;
Which by the Jews long hid, and Disesteem'd,
He heard of by Tradition, and redeem'd.
But were he not in this black habit deck't,
This half transparent Man would soon reflect
Each colour that he past by; and be seen,
As the Chamelion, yellow, blew, or green.
He drest, and ready to disfurnish now
His Chamber, whose compactness did allow
No empty place for complementing doubt,
But who came last is forc'd first to go out;
I meet one on the Stairs who made me stand,
Stopping the passage, and did him demand:
I answer'd he is here Sir; but you see
You cannot pass to him but thorow me.
He thought himself affronted; and reply'd,
I whom the Pallace never has deny'd
Will make the way here; I said Sir you'l do
Me a great favour, for I seek to go.
He gathring fury still made sign to draw;
But himself there clos'd in a Scabbard saw
As narrow as his Sword's; and I, that was
Delightful, said there can no Body pass

Except by penetration hither, where
Two make a crowd, nor can three Persons here
Consist but in one substance. Then, to fit
Our peace, the Priest said I too had some wit:
To prov't, I said, the place doth us invite
But its own narrowness, Sir, to unite.
He ask'd me pardon; and to make me way
Went down, as I him follow'd to obey.
But the propitiatory Priest had straight
Oblig'd us, when below, to celebrate
Together our attonement: so increas'd
Betwixt us two the Dinner to a Feast.
Let it suffice that we could eat in peace;
And that both Poems did and Quarrels cease
During the Table; though my new made Friend
Did, as he threatned, ere 'twere long intend
To be both witty and valiant: I loth,
Said 'twas too late, he was already both.
But now, Alas, my first Tormentor came,
Who satisfy'd with eating, but not tame
Turns to recite; though Judges most severe
After th'Assizes dinner mild appear,
And on full stomach do condemn but few:
Yet he more strict my sentence doth renew;
And draws out of the black box of his Breast
Ten quire of paper in which he was drest.
Yet that which was a greater cruelty
Then Nero's Poem he calls charity:
And so the Pelican at his door hung
Picks out the tender bosome to its young.
Of all his Poems there he stands ungirt
Save only two foul copies for his shirt:
Yet these he promises as soon as clean.
But how I loath'd to see my Neighbour glean
Those papers, which he pilled from within
Like white fleaks rising from a Leaper's skin!
More odious then those raggs which the French youth
At ordinaries after dinner show'th,
When they compare their Chancres and Poulains.
Yet he first kist them, and after takes pains
To read; and then, because he understood good.
Not one Word, thought and swore that they were
But all his praises could not now appease
The provok't Author, whom it did displease
To hear his Verses, by so just a curse,
That were ill made condemn'd to be read worse:
And how (impossible) he made yet more
Absurdityes in them then were before.
For he his untun'd voice did fall or raise
As a deaf Man upon a Viol playes,
Making the half points and the periods run

Confus'der then the atomes in the Sun.
Thereat the Poet swell'd, with anger full,
And roar'd out, like Perillus in's own Bull;
Sir you read false. That any one but you
Should know the contrary. Whereat, I, now
Made Mediator, in my room, said, Why?
To say that you read false Sir is no Lye.
Thereat the waxen Youth relented straight;
But saw with sad dispair that was too late.
For the disdainful Poet was retir'd
Home, his most furious Satyr to have fir'd
Against the Rebel; who, at this struck dead
Wept bitterly as disinherited.
Who should commend his Mistress now? Or who
Praise him? both difficult indeed to do
With truth. I counsell'd him to go in time,
Ere the fierce Poets anger turn'd to rime.
He hasted; and I, finding my self free,
Did, as he threatned, ere 'twere long intend
As one scap't strangely from Captivity,
Have made the Chance be painted; and go now
To hang it in Saint Peter's for a Vow.

Upon Appleton House, To My Lord Fairfax
Within this sober Frame expect
Work of no Forrain Architect;
That unto Caves the Quarries drew,
And Forrests did to Pastures hew;
Who of his great Design in pain
Did for a Model vault his Brain,
Whose Columnes should so high be rais'd
To arch the Brows that on them gaz'd.

Why should of all things Man unrul'd
Such unproportion'd dwellings build?
The Beasts are by their Denns exprest:
And Birds contrive an equal Nest;
The low roof'd Tortoises do dwell
In cases fit of Tortoise-shell:
No Creature loves an empty space;
Their Bodies measure out their Place.

But He, superfluously spread,
Demands more room alive then dead.
And in his hollow Palace goes
Where Winds as he themselves may lose.
What need of all this Marble Crust
T'impark the wanton Mose of Dust,
That thinks by Breadth the World t'unite

Though the first Builders fail'd in Height?

But all things are composed here
Like Nature, orderly and near:
In which we the Dimensions find
Of that more sober Age and Mind,
When larger sized Men did stoop
To enter at a narrow loop;
As practising, in doors so strait,
To strain themselves through Heavens Gate.

And surely when the after Age
Shall hither come in Pilgrimage,
These sacred Places to adore,
By Vere and Fairfax trod before,
Men will dispute how their Extent
Within such dwarfish Confines went:
And some will smile at this, as well
As Romulus his Bee-like Cell.

Humility alone designs
Those short but admirable Lines,
By which, ungirt and unconstrain'd,
Things greater are in less contain'd.
Let others vainly strive t'immure
The Circle in the Quadrature!
These holy Mathematics can
In ev'ry Figure equal Man.

Yet thus the laden House does sweat,
And scarce indures the Master great:
But where he comes the swelling Hall
Stirs, and the Square grows Spherical;
More by his Magnitude distrest,
Then he is by its straitness prest:
And too officiously it slights
That in it self which him delights.

So Honour better Lowness bears,
Then That unwonted Greatness wears
Height with a certain Grace does bend,
But low Things clownishly ascend.
And yet what needs there here Excuse,
Where ev'ry Thing does answer Use?
Where neatness nothing can condemn,
Nor Pride invent what to contemn?

A Stately Frontispice Of Poor
Adorns without the open Door:
Nor less the Rooms within commends
Daily new Furniture Of Friends.

The House was built upon the Place
Only as for a Mark Of Grace;
And for an Inn to entertain
Its Lord a while, but not remain.

Him Bishops-Hill, or Denton may,
Or Bilbrough, better hold then they:
But Nature here hath been so free
As if she said leave this to me.
Art would more neatly have defac'd
What she had laid so sweetly wast;
In fragrant Gardens, shaddy Woods,
Deep Meadows, and transparent Floods.

While with slow Eyes we these survey,
And on each pleasant footstep stay,
We opportunly may relate
The progress of this Houses Fate.
A Nunnery first gave it birth.
For Virgin Buildings oft brought forth.
And all that Neighbour-Ruine shows
The Quarries whence this dwelling rose.

Near to this gloomy Cloysters Gates
There dwelt the blooming Virgin Thwates,
Fair beyond Measure, and an Heir
Which might Deformity make fair.
And oft She spent the Summer Suns
Discoursing with the Suttle Nuns.
Whence in these Words one to her weav'd,
(As 'twere by Chance) Thoughts long conceiv'd.

"Within this holy leisure we
"Live innocently as you see.
"these Walls restrain the World without,
"But hedge our Liberty about.
"These Bars inclose the wider Den
"Of those wild Creatures, called Men.
"The Cloyster outward shuts its Gates,
"And, from us, locks on them the Grates.

"Here we, in shining Armour white,
"Like Virgin Amazons do fight.
"And our chast Lamps we hourly trim,
"Lest the great Bridegroom find them dim.
"Our Orient Breaths perfumed are
"With insense of incessant Pray'r.
"And Holy-water of our Tears
"Most strangly our complexion clears.

"Not Tears of Grief; but such as those

"With which calm Pleasure overflows;
"Or Pity, when we look on you
"That live without this happy Vow.
"How should we grieve that must be seen
"Each one a Spouse, and each a Queen;
"And can in Heaven hence behold
"Our brighter Robes and Crowns of Gold?

"When we have prayed all our Beads,
"Some One the holy Legend reads;
"While all the rest with Needles paint
"The Face and Graces of the Saint.
"But what the Linnen can't receive
"They in their Lives do interweave
"This work the Saints best represents;
"That serves for Altar's Ornaments.

"But much it to our work would add
"If here your hand, your Face we had:
"By it we would our Lady touch;
"Yet thus She you resembles much.
"Some of your Features, as we sow'd,
"Through ev'ry Shrine should be bestow'd.
"And in one Beauty we would take
"Enough a thousand Saints to make.

"And (for I dare not quench the Fire
"That me does for your good inspire)
"'Twere Sacriledge a Mant t'admit
"To holy things, for Heaven fit.
"I see the Angels in a Crown
"On you the Lillies show'ring down:
"And round about you Glory breaks,
"That something more then humane speaks.

"All Beauty, when at such a height,
"Is so already consecrate.
"Fairfax I know; and long ere this
"Have mark'd the Youth, and what he is.
"But can he such a Rival seem
"For whom you Heav'n should disesteem?
"Ah, no! and 'twould more Honour prove
"He your Devoto were, then Love.

Here live beloved, and obey'd:
Each one your Sister, each your Maid.
"And, if our Rule seem strictly pend,
"The Rule it self to you shall bend.
"Our Abbess too, now far in Age,
"Doth your succession near presage.
"How soft the yoke on us would lye,

"Might such fair Hands as yours it tye!

"Your voice, the sweetest of the Quire,
"Shall draw Heav'n nearer, raise us higher.
"And your Example, if our Head,
"Will soon us to perfection lead.
"Those Virtues to us all so dear,
"Will straight grow Sanctity when here:
"And that, once sprung, increase so fast
"Till Miracles it work at last.

"Nor is our Order yet so nice,
"Delight to banish as a Vice.
"Here Pleasure Piety doth meet;
"One perfecting the other Sweet.
"So through the mortal fruit we boyl
"The Sugars uncorrupting Oyl:
"And that which perisht while we pull,
"Is thus preserved clear and full.

"For such indeed are all our Arts;
"Still handling Natures finest Parts.
"Flow'rs dress the Altars; for the Clothes,
"The Sea-born Amber we compose;
"Balms for the griv'd we draw; and pasts
"We mold, as Baits for curious tasts.
"What need is here of Man? unless
"These as sweet Sins we should confess.

"Each Night among us to your side
"Appoint a fresh and Virgin Bride;
"Whom if Our Lord at midnight find,
"Yet Neither should be left behind.
"Where you may lye as chast in Bed,
"As Pearls together billeted.
"All Night embracing Arm in Arm,
"Like Chrystal pure with Cotton warm.

"But what is this to all the store
"Of Joys you see, and may make more!
"Try but a while, if you be wise:
"The Tryal neither Costs, nor Tyes.
Now Fairfax seek her promis'd faith:
Religion that dispensed hath;
Which She hence forward does begin;
The Nuns smooth Tongue has suckt her in.

Oft, though he knew it was in vain,
Yet would he valiantly complain.
"Is this that Sanctity so great,
"An Art by which you finly'r cheat

"Hypocrite Witches, hence Avant,
"Who though in prison yet inchant!
"Death only can such Theeves make fast,
"As rob though in the Dungeon cast.

"Were there but, when this House was made,
"One Stone that a just Hand had laid,
"It must have fall'n upon her Head
"Who first Thee from thy Faith misled.
"And yet, how well soever ment,
"With them 'twould soon grow fraudulent
"For like themselves they alter all,
"And vice infects the very Wall.

"But sure those Buildings last not long,
"Founded by Folly, kept by Wrong.
"I know what Fruit their Gardens yield,
"When they it think by Night conceal'd.
"Fly from their Vices. 'Tis thy state,
"Not Thee, that they would consecrate.
"Fly from their Ruine. How I fear
"Though guiltless lest thou perish there.

What should he do? He would respect
Religion, but not Right neglect:
For first Religion taught him Right,
And dazled not but clear'd his sight.
Sometimes resolv'd his Sword he draws,
But reverenceth then the Laws:
"For Justice still that Courage led;
First from a Judge, then Souldier bred.

Small Honour would be in the Storm.
The Court him grants the lawful Form;
Which licens'd either Peace or Force,
To hinder the unjust Divorce.
Yet still the Nuns his Right debar'd,
Standing upon their holy Guard.
Ill-counsell'd Women, do you know
Whom you resist, or what you do?

Is not this he whose Offspring fierce
Shall fight through all the Universe;
And with successive Valour try
France, Poland, either Germany;
Till one, as long since prophecy'd,
His Horse through conquer'd Britain ride?
Yet, against Fate, his Spouse they kept;
And the great Race would intercept.

Some to the Breach against their Foes

Their Wooden Saints in vain oppose
Another bolder stands at push
With their old Holy-Water Brush.
While the disjointed Abbess threads
The gingling Chain-shot of her Beads.
But their lowd'st Cannon were their Lungs;
And sharpest Weapons were their Tongues.

But, waving these aside like Flyes,
Young Fairfax through the Wall does rise.
Then th' unfrequented Vault appear'd,
And superstitions vainly fear'd.
The Relicks False were set to view;
Only the Jewels there were true.
But truly bright and holy Thwaites
That weeping at the Altar waites.

But the glad Youth away her bears,
And to the Nuns bequeaths her Tears:
Who guiltily their Prize bemoan,
Like Gipsies that a Child hath stoln.
Thenceforth (as when th' Inchantment ends
The Castle vanishes or rends)
The wasting Cloister with the rest
Was in one instant dispossest.

At the demolishing, this Seat
To Fairfax fell as by Escheat.
And what both Nuns and Founders will'd
'Tis likely better thus fulfill'd,
For if the Virgin prov'd not theirs,
The Cloyster yet remained hers.
Though many a Nun there made her vow,
'Twas no Religious-House till now.

From that blest Bed the Heroe came,
Whom France and Poland yet does fame:
Who, when retired here to Peace,
His warlike Studies could not cease;
But laid these Gardens out in sport
In the just Figure of a Fort;
And with five Bastions it did fence,
As aiming one for ev'ry Sense.

When in the East the Morning Ray
Hangs out the Colours of the Day,
The Bee through these known Allies hums,
Beating the Dian with its Drumms.
Then Flow'rs their drowsie Eylids raise,
Their Silken Ensigns each displayes,
And dries its Pan yet dank with Dew,

And fills its Flask with Odours new.

These, as their Governour goes by,
In fragrant Vollyes they let fly;
And to salute their Governess
Again as great a charge they press:
None for the Virgin Nymph; for She
Seems with the Flow'rs a Flow'r to be.
And think so still! though not compare
With Breath so sweet, or Cheek so faire.

Well shot ye Fireman! Oh how sweet,
And round your equal Fires do meet;
Whose shrill report no Ear can tell,
But Ecchoes to the Eye and smell.
See how the Flow'rs, as at Parade,
Under their Colours stand displaid:
Each Regiment in order grows,
That of the Tulip Pinke and Rose.

But when the vigilant Patroul
Of Stars walks round about the Pole,
Their Leaves, that to the stalks are curl'd,
Seem to their Staves the Ensigns furl'd.
Then in some Flow'rs beloved Hut
Each Bee as Sentinel is shut;
And sleeps so too: but, if once stir'd,
She runs you through, or askes The Word.

Oh Thou, that dear and happy Isle
The Garden of the World ere while,
Thou Paradise of four Seas,
Which Heaven planted us to please,
But, to exclude the World, did guard
With watry if not flaming Sword;
What luckless Apple did we tast,
To make us Mortal, and The Wast.

Unhappy! shall we never more
That sweet Milltia restore,
When Gardens only had their Towrs,
And all the Garrisons were Flow'rs,
When Roses only Arms might bear,
And Men did rosie Garlands wear?
Tulips, in several Colours barr'd,
Were then the Switzers of our Guard.

The Gardiner had the Souldiers place,
And his more gentle Forts did trace.
The Nursery of all things green
Was then the only Magazeen.

The Winter Quarters were the Stoves,
Where he the tender Plants removes.
But War all this doth overgrow:
We Ord'nance Plant and Powder sow.

And yet their walks one on the Sod
Who, had it pleased him and God,
Might once have made our Gardens spring
Fresh as his own and flourishing.
But he preferr'd to the Cinque Ports
These five imaginary Forts:
And, in those half-dry Trenches, spann'd
Pow'r which the Ocean might command.

For he did, with his utmost Skill,
Ambition weed, but Conscience till.
Conscience, that Heaven-nursed Plant,
Which most our Earthly Gardens want.
A prickling leaf it bears, and such
As that which shrinks at ev'ry touch;
But Flow'rs eternal, and divine,
That in the Crowns of Saints do shine.

The sight does from these Bastions ply,
Th' invisible Artilery;
And at proud Cawood Castle seems
To point the Battery of its Beams.
As if it quarrell'd in the Seat
Th' Ambition of its Prelate great.
But ore the Meads below it plays,
Or innocently seems to gaze.

And now to the Abbyss I pass
Of that unfathomable Grass,
Where Men like Grashoppers appear,
But Grashoppers are Gyants there:
They, in there squeking Laugh, contemn
Us as we walk more low then them:
And, from the Precipices tall
Of the green spir's, to us do call.

To see Men through this Meadow Dive,
We wonder how they rise alive.
As, under Water, none does know
Whether he fall through it or go.
But, as the Marriners that sound,
And show upon their Lead the Ground,
They bring up Flow'rs so to be seen,
And prove they've at the Bottom been.

No Scene that turns with Engines strange

Does oftner then these Meadows change,
For when the Sun the Grass hath vext,
The tawny Mowers enter next;
Who seem like Israaliies to be,
Walking on foot through a green Sea.
To them the Grassy Deeps divide,
And crowd a Lane to either Side.

With whistling Sithe, and Elbow strong,
These Massacre the Grass along:
While one, unknowing, carves the Rail,
Whose yet unfeather'd Quils her fail.
The Edge all bloody from its Breast
He draws, and does his stroke detest;
Fearing the Flesh untimely mow'd
To him a Fate as black forebode.

But bloody Thestylis, that waites
To bring the mowing Camp their Cates,
Greedy as Kites has trust it up,
And forthwith means on it to sup:
When on another quick She lights,
And cryes, he call'd us Israelites;
But now, to make his saying true,
Rails rain for Quails, for Manna Dew.

Unhappy Birds! what does it boot
To build below the Grasses Root;
When Lowness is unsafe as Hight,
And Chance o'retakes what scapeth spight?
And now your Orphan Parents Call
Sounds your untimely Funeral.
Death-Trumpets creak in such a Note,
And 'tis the Sourdine in their Throat.

Or sooner hatch or higher build:
The Mower now commands the Field;
In whose new Traverse seemeth wrought
A Camp of Battail newly fought:
Where, as the Meads with Hay, the Plain
Lyes quilted ore with Bodies slain:
The Women that with forks it filing,
Do represent the Pillaging.

And now the careless Victors play,
Dancing the Triumphs of the Hay;
Where every Mowers wholesome Heat
Smells like an Alexanders Sweat.
Their Females fragrant as the Mead
Which they in Fairy Circles tread:
When at their Dances End they kiss,

Their new-made Hay not sweeter is.

When after this 'tis pil'd in Cocks,
Like a calm Sea it shews the Rocks:
We wondring in the River near
How Boats among them safely steer.
Or, like the Desert Memphis Sand,
Short Pyramids of Hay do stand.
And such the Roman Camps do rise
In Hills for Soldiers Obsequies.

This Scene again withdrawing brings
A new and empty Face of things;
A levell'd space, as smooth and plain,
As Clothes for Lilly strecht to stain.
The World when first created sure
Was such a Table rase and pure.
Or rather such is the Toril
Ere the Bulls enter at Madril.

For to this naked equal Flat,
Which Levellers take Pattern at,
The Villagers in common chase
Their Cattle, which it closer rase;
And what below the Sith increast
Is pincht yet nearer by the Breast.
Such, in the painted World, appear'd
Davenant with th'Universal Heard.

They seem within the polisht Grass
A landskip drawen in Looking-Glass.
And shrunk in the huge Pasture show
As spots, so shap'd, on Faces do.
Such Fleas, ere they approach the Eye,
In Multiplyiug Glasses lye.
They feed so wide, so slowly move,
As Constellatious do above.

Then, to conclude these pleasant Acts,
Denton sets ope its Cataracts;
And makes the Meadow truly be
(What it but seem'd before) a Sea.
For, jealous of its Lords long stay,
It try's t'invite him thus away.
The River in it self is drown'd,
And Isl's th' astonish Cattle round.

Let others tell the Paradox,
How Eels now bellow in the Ox;
How Horses at their Tails do kick,
Turn'd as they hang to Leeches quick;

How Boats can over Bridges sail;
And Fishes do the Stables scale.
How Salmons trespassing are found;
And Pikes are taken in the Pound.

But I, retiring from the Flood,
Take Sanctuary in the Wood;
And, while it lasts, my self imbark
In this yet green, yet growing Ark;
Where the first Carpenter might best
Fit Timber for his Keel have Prest.
And where all Creatures might have shares,
Although in Armies, not in Paires.

The double Wood of ancient Stocks
Link'd in so thick, an Union locks,
It like two Pedigrees appears,
On one hand Fairfax, th' other Veres:
Of whom though many fell in War,
Yet more to Heaven shooting are:
And, as they Natures Cradle deckt,
Will in green Age her Hearse expect.

When first the Eye this Forrest sees
It seems indeed as Wood not Trees:
As if their Neighbourhood so old
To one great Trunk them all did mold.
There the huge Bulk takes place, as ment
To thrust up a Fifth Element;
And stretches still so closely wedg'd
As if the Night within were hedg'd.

Dark all without it knits; within
It opens passable and thin;
And in as loose an order grows,
As the Corinthean Porticoes.
The Arching Boughs unite between
The Columnes of the Temple green;
And underneath the winged Quires
Echo about their tuned Fires.

The Nightingale does here make choice
To sing the Tryals of her Voice.
Low Shrubs she sits in, and adorns
With Musick high the squatted Thorns.
But highest Oakes stoop down to hear,
And listning Elders prick the Ear.
The Thorn, lest it should hurt her, draws
Within the Skin its shrunken claws.

But I have for my Musick found

A Sadder, yet more pleasing Sound:
The Stock-doves whose fair necks are grac'd
With Nuptial Rings their Ensigns chast;
Yet always, for some Cause unknown,
Sad pair unto the Elms they moan.
O why should such a Couple mourn,
That in so equal Flames do burn!

Then as I carless on the Bed
Of gelid Straw-berryes do tread,
And through the Hazles thick espy
The hatching Thrastles shining Eye,
The Heron from the Ashes top,
The eldest of its young lets drop,
As if it Stork-like did pretend
That Tribute to its Lord to send.

But most the Hewel's wonders are,
Who here has the Holt-felsters care.
He walks still upright from the Root,
Meas'ring the Timber with his Foot;
And all the way, to keep it clean,
Doth from the Bark the Wood-moths glean.
He, with his Beak, examines well
Which fit to stand and which to fell.

The good he numbers up, and hacks;
As if he mark'd them with the Ax.
But where he, tinkling with his Beak,
Does find the hollow Oak to speak,
That for his building he designs,
And through the tainted Side he mines.
Who could have thought the tallest Oak
Should fall by such a feeble Strok'!

Nor would it, had the Tree not fed
A Traitor-worm, within it bred.
(As first our Flesh corrupt within
Tempts impotent and bashful Sin.
And yet that Worm triumphs not long,
But serves to feed the Hewels young.
While the Oake seems to fall content,
Viewing the Treason's Punishment.

Thus I, easie Philosopher,
Among the Birds and Trees confer:
And little now to make me, wants
Or of the Fowles, or of the Plants.
Give me but Wings as they, and I
Streight floting on the Air shall fly:
Or turn me but, and you shall see

I was but an inverted Tree.

Already I begin to call
In their most-learned Original:
And where I Language want,my Signs
The Bird upon the Bough divines;
And more attentive there doth sit
Then if She were with Lime-twigs knit.
No Leaf does tremble in the Wind
Which I returning cannot find.

Out of these scatter'd Sibyls Leaves
Strange Prophecies my Phancy weaves:
And in one History consumes,
Like Mexique Paintings, all the Plumes.
What Rome, Greece, Palestine, ere said
I in this light Mosaick read.
Thrice happy he who, not mistook,
Hath read in Natures mystick Book.

And see how Chance's better Wit
Could with a Mask my studies hit!
The Oak-Leaves me embroyder all,
Between which Caterpillars crawl:
And Ivy, with familiar trails,
Me licks, and clasps, and curles, and hales.
Under this antick Cope I move
Like some great Prelate of the Grove,

Then, languishing with ease, I toss
On Pallets swoln of Velvet Moss;
While the Wind, cooling through the Boughs,
Flatters with Air my panting Brows.
Thanks for my Rest ye Mossy Banks,
And unto you cool Zephyr's Thanks,
Who, as my Hair, my Thoughts too shed,
And winnow from the Chaff my Head.

How safe, methinks, and strong, behind
These Trees have I incamp'd my Mind;
Where Beauty, aiming at the Heart,
Bends in some Tree its useless Dart;
And where the World no certain Shot
Can make, or me it toucheth not.
But I on it securely play,
And gaul its Horsemen all the Day.

Bind me ye Woodbines in your 'twines,
Curle me about ye gadding Vines,
And Oh so close your Circles lace,
That I may never leave this Place:

But, lest your Fetters prove too weak,
Ere I your Silken Bondage break,
Do you, O Brambles, chain me too,
And courteous Briars nail me though.

Here in the Morning tye my Chain,
Where the two Woods have made a Lane;
While, like a Guard on either side,
The Trees before their Lord divide;
This, like a long and equal Thread,
Betwixt two Labyrinths does lead.
But, where the Floods did lately drown,
There at the Ev'ning stake me down.

For now the Waves are fal'n and dry'd,
And now the Meadows fresher dy'd;
Whose Grass, with moister colour dasht,
Seems as green Silks but newly washt.
No Serpent new nor Crocodile
Remains behind our little Nile;
Unless it self you will mistake,
Among these Meads the only Snake.

See in what wanton harmless folds
It ev'ry where the Meadow holds;
And its yet muddy back doth lick,
Till as a Chrystal Mirrour slick;
Where all things gaze themselves, and doubt
If they be in it or without.
And for his shade which therein shines,
Narcissus like, the Sun too pines.

Oh what a Pleasure 'tis to hedge
My Temples here with heavy sedge;
Abandoning my lazy Side,
Stretcht as a Bank unto the Tide;
Or to suspend my sliding Foot
On the Osiers undermined Root,
And in its Branches tough to hang,
While at my Lines the Fishes twang!

But now away my Hooks, my Quills,
And Angles, idle Utensils.
The Young Maria walks to night:
Hide trifling Youth thy Pleasures slight.
'Twere shame that such judicious Eyes
Should with such Toyes a Man surprize;
She that already is the Law
Of all her Sex, her Ages Aw.

See how loose Nature, in respect

To her, it self doth recollect;
And every thing so whisht and fine,
Starts forth with to its Bonne Mine.
The Sun himself, of Her aware,
Seems to descend with greater Care,
And lest She see him go to Bed,
In blushing Clouds conceales his Head.

So when the Shadows laid asleep
From underneath these Banks do creep,
And on the River as it flows
With Eben Shuts begin to close;
The modest Halcyon comes in sight,
Flying betwixt the Day and Night;
And such an horror calm and dumb,
Admiring Nature does benum.

The viscous Air, wheres'ere She fly,
Follows and sucks her Azure dy;
The gellying Stream compacts below,
If it might fix her shadow so;
The Stupid Fishes hang, as plain
As Flies in Chrystal overt'ane,
And Men the silent Scene assist,
Charm'd with the saphir-winged Mist.

Maria such, and so doth hush
The World, and through the Ev'ning rush.
No new-born Comet such a Train
Draws through the Skie, nor Star new-slain.
For streight those giddy Rockets fail,
Which from the putrid Earth exhale,
But by her Flames, in Heaven try'd,
Nature is wholly Vitrifi'd.

'Tis She that to these Gardens gave
That wondrous Beauty which they have;
She streightness on the Woods bestows;
To Her the Meadow sweetness owes;
Nothing could make the River be
So Chrystal-pure but only She;
She yet more Pure, Sweet, Streight, and Fair,
Then Gardens, Woods, Meads, Rivers are.

Therefore what first She on them spent,
They gratefully again present.
The Meadow Carpets where to tread;
The Garden Flow'rs to Crown Her Head;
And for a Glass the limpid Brook,
Where She may all her Beautyes look;
But, since She would not have them seen,

The Wood about her draws a Skreen.

For She, to higher Beauties rais'd,
Disdains to be for lesser prais'd.
She counts her Beauty to converse
In all the Languages as hers;
Not yet in those her self imployes
But for the Wisdome, not the Noyse;
Nor yet that Wisdome would affect,
But as 'tis Heavens Dialect.

Blest Nymph! that couldst so soon prevent
Those Trains by Youth against thee meant;
Tears (watry Shot that pierce the Mind;)
And Sighs (Loves Cannon charg'd with Wind;)
True Praise (That breaks through all defence;)
And feign'd complying Innocence;
But knowing where this Ambush lay,
She scap'd the safe, but roughest Way.

This 'tis to have been from the first
In a Domestick Heaven nurst,
Under the Discipline severe
Of Fairfax, and the starry Vere;
Where not one object can come nigh
But pure, and spotless as the Eye;
And Goodness doth it self intail
On Females, if there want a Male.

Go now fond Sex that on your Face
Do all your useless Study place,
Nor once at Vice your Brows dare knit
Lest the smooth Forehead wrinkled sit
Yet your own Face shall at you grin,
Thorough the Black-bag of your Skin;
When knowledge only could have fill'd
And Virtue all those Furows till'd.

Hence She with Graces more divine
Supplies beyond her Sex the Line;
And, like a sprig of Misleto,
On the Fairfacian Oak does grow;
Whence, for some universal good,
The Priest shall cut the sacred Bud;
While her glad Parents most rejoice,
And make their Destiny their Choice.

Mean time ye Fields, Springs, Bushes, Flow'rs,
Where yet She leads her studious Hours,
(Till Fate her worthily translates,
And find a Fairfax for our Thwaites)

Employ the means you have by Her,
And in your kind your selves preferr;
That, as all Virgins She preceds,
So you all Woods, Streams, Gardens, Meads.

For you Thessalian Tempe's Seat
Shall now be scorn'd as obsolete;
Aranjeuz, as less, disdain'd;
The Bel-Retiro as constrain'd;
But name not the Idalian Grove,
For 'twas the Seat of wanton Love;
Much less the Dead's Elysian Fields,
Yet nor to them your Beauty yields.

'Tis not, what once it was, the World;
But a rude heap together hurl'd;
All negligently overthrown,
Gulfes, Deserts, Precipices, Stone.
Your lesser World contains the same.
But in more decent Order tame;
You Heaven's Center, Nature's Lap.
And Paradice's only Map.

But now the Salmon-Fishers moist
Their Leathern Boats begin to hoist;
And, like Antipodes in Shoes,
Have shod their Heads in their Canoos.
How Tortoise like, but not so slow,
These rational Amphibii go?
Let's in: for the dark Hemisphere
Does now like one of them appear.

The Statue At Charing Cross
I.
What can be the mystery why Charing-Crosse
This five months continues still muffled with board?
Dear Wheeler, impart; we are all at a losse,
Unless we must have Punchinello restored.

II.
Twere to Scaramouchio too great disrespect.
To limit his troop to this theatre small,
Besides the injustice it were to eject
That mimick, so legally seized of WhitehalL

III.
For a diall the place is too unsecure,
Since the Privy-Grarden could not it defend;
And so near to the Court they will never endure

Any monument, how they their time may mispend.

IV.
Were these deales yet in store for sheathing our Fleet,
When the King in armada to Portsmouth should saile,
Or the Bishops and Treasurer, did they agree't
To repair with such riff-raff our churche's old pale?

V.
No; to comfort the heart of the poor cavalier,
The late King on horseback is here to be shown;
What ad<^with your Kings and your statues is here!
Have we not had enough, pray, already of one?

VI.
Does the Treasurer think men so loyally tame.
When their pensions are stop'd, to be fool'd with a sight?
And 'tis forty to one, if he play the old game,
He'll reduce us e'er long to rehearse forty-eight.

VII.
The Trojan horse, so, (not of brass, but of wood)
Had within it an army that burnt down the town;
However, 'tis ominous, if understood,
For the old King on horseback is but an Half-crowne.

VIII.
Yet, his brother-in-law's horse had gain'd such repute.
That the Treasurer thought prudent to try it again;
And, instead of that Market of herbs and of fruit,
He will here keep a Shambles of Parliament Men.

IX.
But why is the work then so long at a stand?
Such things you should never — or suddenly do:
As the Parliament twice was prorogued by your hand,
Would you venture so farr to prorogue the King too?

X.
Let's have a King, sir, be he new, be he old,
Not Vyner delay'd us so, though he were broken;
Tho' the King be of copper, and Danby of gold,
Shall the Treasurer of guineas refuse such a token?

XI.
The housewifery treasuress sure is grown nice,
And so liberally treated the members at supper;
She thinks not convenient to go to the price.
And we've lost both our King, and our horse, and his crupper.

XII.

Where so many parties there are to provide.
To buy a King is not so wise as to sell;
And however, she said, it could not be denied,
That a monarch of gingerbread might do as well.

XIII.
But the Treasurer told her, he thought she was mad.
And his Parliament list too withall did produce;
When he shew'd her, that so many voters he had,
As would the next tax reimburse them with use.

XIV.
So the statue will up after all this delay,
But to turn the face towards Whitehall you must shun;
Though of brass, yet with grief it would melt him away,
To behold such a prodigal Court and a son.

Young Love
Come little Infant, Love me now,
While thine unsuspected years
Clear thine aged Fathers brow
From cold Jealousie and Fears.

Pretty surely 'twere to see
By young Love old Time beguil'd:
While our Sportings are as free
As the Nurses with the Child.

Common Beauties stay fifteen;
Such as yours should swifter move;
Whole fair Blossoms are too green
Yet for lust, but not for Love.

Love as much the snowy Lamb
Or the wanton Kid does prize,
As the lusty Bull or Ram,
For his morning Sacrifice.

Now then love me: time may take
Thee before thy time away:
Of this Need wee'l Virtue make,
And learn Love before we may.

So we win of doubtful Fate;
And, if good she to us meant,
We that Good shall antedate,
Or, if ill, that Ill prevent.

Thus as Kingdomes, frustrating

Other Titles to their Crown,
In the craddle crown their King,
So all Forraign Claims to drown.

So, to make all Rivals vain,
Now I crown thee with my Love:
Crown me with thy Love again,
And we both shall Monarchs prove.

Upon The Hill And Grove At Billborow
To the Lord Fairfax.

See how the arched Earth does here
Rise in a perfect Hemisphere!
The stiffest Compass could not strike
A line more circular and like;
Nor softest Pensel draw a Brow.
So equal as this Hill does bow.
It seems as for a Model laid,
And that the World by it was made.

Here learn ye Mountains more unjust,
Which to abrupter greatness thrust,
That do with your hook-shoulder'd height
The Earth deform and Heaven frght.
For whose excrescence ill design'd,
Nature must a new Center find,
Learn here those humble steps to tread,
Which to securer Glory lead.

See what a soft access and wide
Lyes open to its grassy side;
Nor with the rugged path deterrs
The feet of breathless Travellers.
See then how courteous it ascends,
And all the way ir rises bends;
Nor for it self the height does gain,
But only strives to raise the Plain.

Yet thus it all the field commands,
And in unenvy'd Greatness stands,
Discerning furthe then the Cliff
Of Heaven-daring Teneriff.
How glad the weary Seamen hast
When they salute it from the Mast!
By Night the Northern Star their way
Directs, and this no less by Day.

Upon its crest this Mountain grave

A Plum of aged Trees does wave.
No hostile hand durst ere invade
With impious Steel the sacred Shade.
For something alwaies did appear
Of the Great Masters terrour there:
And Men could hear his Armour still
Ratling through all the Grove and Hill.

Fear of the Master, and respect
Of the great Nymph did it protect;
Vera the Nymph that him inspir'd,
To whom he often here retir'd,
And on these Okes ingrav'd her Name;
Such Wounds alone these Woods became:
But ere he well the Barks could part
'Twas writ already in their Heart.

For they ('tis credible) have sense,
As we, of Love and Reverence,
And underneath the Courser Rind
The Genius of the house do bind.
Hence they successes seem to know,
And in their Lord's advancement grow;
But in no Memory were seen
As under this so streight and green.

Yet now no further strive to shoot,
Contented if they fix their Root.
Nor to the winds uncertain gust,
Their prudent Heads too far intrust.
Onely sometimes a flutt'ring Breez
Discourses with the breathing Trees;
Which in their modest Whispers name
Those Acts that swell'd the Cheek of Fame.

Much other Groves, say they, then these
And other Hills him once did please.
Through Groves of Pikes he thunder'd then,
And Mountains rais'd of dying Men.
For all the Civick Garlands due
To him our Branches are but few.
Nor are our Trunks enow to bear
The Trophees of one fertile Year.

'Tis true, the Trees nor ever spoke
More certain Oracles in Oak.
But Peace (if you his favour prize)
That Courage its own Praises flies.
Therefore to your obscurer Seats
From his own Brightness he retreats:
Nor he the Hills without the Groves,

Nor Height but with Retirement loves.

The Fair Singer

To make a final conquest of all me,
Love did compose so sweet an Enemy,
In whom both Beauties to my death agree,
Joyning themselves in fatal Harmony;
That while she with her Eyes my Heart does bind,
She with her Voice might captivate my Mind.

I could have fled from One but singly fair:
My dis-intangled Soul it self might save,
Breaking the curled trammels of her hair.
But how should I avoid to be her Slave,
Whose subtile Art invisibly can wreath
My Fetters of the very Air I breath?

It had been easie fighting in some plain,
Where Victory might hang in equal choice.
But all resistance against her is vain,
Who has th' advantage both of Eyes and Voice.
And all my Forces needs must be undone,
She having gained both the Wind and Sun.

Advice To A Painter

Spread a large canvas, Painter, to contain
The great assembly, and the numerous train;
Where all about him shall in triumph sit,
Abhorring wisdom, and despising wit;
Hating all justice, and resolv'd to fight,
To rob their native country of their right.
First draw his Highness prostrate to the South,
Adoring Rome, this label in his mouth,
"Most holy father! being joyn'd in league
With father Patrick, Danby, and with Teague,
Thrown at your sacred feet, I humbly bow,
I, and the wise associates of my vow,
A vow, nor fire nor sword shall ever end,
Till all this nation to your footstool bend.
Thus arm'd with zeal and blessing from your hands,
I'll raise my Papists, and my Irish bands;
And by a noble well-contrived plot,
Managed by wise Fitz-Gerald, and by Scot,
Prove to the world I'll make old England know,
That Common Sense is my eternal foe.
I ne'er can fight in a more glorious cause,
Than to destroy their liberty and laws;

Their House of Commons, and their House of Lords,
Parliaments, precedents, and dull records.
Shall these e'er dare to contradict my will,
And think a prince o' the blood can e'er do ill!
It is our birthright to have power to kill.
Shall they e'er dare to think they shall decide
The way to heaven! and who shall be my guide?
Shall they pretend to say, that bread is bread,
If we affirm it is a God indeed?
Or there 's no Purgatory for the dead?
That extreme unction is but common oyl?
And not infallible, the Roman soil?
I'll have those villains in our notions rest;
And I do say it, therefore it's the best."
Next, Painter, draw his Mordant by his side,
Conveying his religion and his bride:
He, who long since abjur'd the royal line,
Does now in Popery with his master join.
Then draw the princess with her golden locks,
Hastening to be envenom'd with the pox.
And in her youthful veins receive a wound,
Which sent N[an] H[yde] before her under ground;
The wound of which the tainted Cartaret fades,
Laid up in store for a new set of maids.
Poor princess! born under a sullen star,
To find such welcome when you came so far!
Better some jealous neighbour of your own
Had call'd you to a sound, tho petty throne;
Where 'twixt a wholsome husband and a page,
You might have linger'd out a lazy age,
Than on dull hopes of being here a Queen,
Ere twenty die, and rot before fifteen.
Now, Painter, show us in the blackest dye,
The counsellors of all this villany.
Clifford, who first appeared in humble guise,
Was always thought too gentle, meek, and wise;
But when he came to act upon the stage,
He prov'd the mad Cathegus of our age.
He and his Duke had both too great a mind,
To be by Justice or by Law confined:
Their broiling heads can bear no other sounds.
Then fleets and armies, battles, blood and wounds:
And to destroy our liberty they hope,
By Irish fools, and an old doting Pope.
Next, Talbot must by his great master stand,
Laden with folly, flesh, and ill-got land;
He's of a size indeed to fill a porch.
But ne'er can make a pillar of the church.
His sword is all his argument, not his book;
Altho no scholar, he can act the cook.
And will cut throats again, if he be paid;

In th' Irish shambles he first leam'd the trade.
Then, Painter, shew thy skill, and in fit place
Let's see the nuncio Arundel's sweet face;
Let the beholders by thy art espy
His sense and soul, as squinting as his eye.
Let Bellasis' autumnal face be seen,
Rich with the spoils of a poor Algerine;
Who, trusting in him, was by him betrayed,
And so shall we, when his advic's obey'd.
The hero once got honour by his sword;
He got his wealth, by breaking of his word;
And now his daughter he hath got with child,
And pimps to have his family defil'd.
Next, Painter, draw the rabble of the plot;
German, Fitz-Gerald, Loffcus, Porter, Scot:
These are fit heads indeed to turn a State,
And change the order of a nation's fate;
Ten thousand such as these shall ne'er control
The smallest atom of an English soul.
Old England on its strong foundation stands,
Defying all their heads and all their hands;
Its steady basis never could be shook,
When wiser men her ruin undertook;
And can her guardian angel let her stoop
At last to madmen, fools, and to the Pope?
No, Painter, no! close up the piece, and see
This crowd of traytors hang'd in effigie.
To the King.

Great Charles, who full of mercy migh'st command,
In peace and pleasure, this thy native Land,
At last take pity of thy tottering throne,
Shook by the faults of others, not thine own;
Let not thy life and crown together end, 105
Destroyed by a false brother and false Mend.
Observe the danger that appears so near,
That all your subjects do each minute fear:
One drop of poyson, or a popish knife,
Ends all the joys of England with thy life.
Brothers, 'tis true, by nature should be kind;
But a too zealous and ambitious mind,
Brib'd with a crown on earth, and one above.
Harbours no friendship, tenderness, or love.
See in all ages what examples are
Of monarchs murder'd by th' impatient heir.
Hard fate of princes, who will ne'er believe.
Till the stroke's struck which they can ne'er retrieve!

Farther Instructions To A Painter.

Painter, once more thy pencil reassume,
And draw me, in one scene, London and Rome:
Here holy Charles, there good Aurelius sat,
Weeping to see their sons degenerate;
His Romans taking up the teemer's trade,
The Britons jigging it in masquerade;
Whilst the brave youths, tir'd with the toil of State,
Their wearied minds and limbs to recreate,
Do to their more belov'd delights repair.
One to his - the other to his player.
Then change the scene, and let the next present
A landscape of our motly Parliament;
And place, hard by the bar, on the left hand,
Circean Clifford with his charming wand;
Our pig-eyed - on his fashion
Set by the worst attorny of our nation:
This great triumvirate that can divide
The spoils of England; and along that side
Place Falstaff's regiment of thredbare coats,
All looking this way, how to give their votes;
And of his dear reward let none despair,
For mony comes when Sey[mou]r leaves the chair.
Change once again, and let the next afford
The figure of a motly council-board
At Arlington's, and round about it sat
Our mighty masters in a warm debate.
Full bowls of lusty wine make them repeat,
To make them t'other council-board forget
That while the King of France with powerful arms,
Gives all his fearful neighbours strange alarms,
We in our glorious bacchanals dispose
The humbled fate of a plebean nose;
Which to effect, when thus it was decreed,
Draw me a champion mounted on a steed;
And after him a brave brigade of horse,
Arm'd at all points, ready to reenforce
His; this assault upon a single man.

'Tis this must make O'Bryon great in story.
And add more beams to Sandys' former glory.
Draw our Olympia next, in council sate
With Cupid, S[eymou]r, and the tool of State:
Two of the first recanters of the house,
That aim at mountains, and bring forth a mouse;
Who make it, by their mean retreat, appear
Five members need not be demanded here.
These must assist her in her countermines,
To overthrow the Derby-House designs;
Whilst Positive walks, like woodcock in the park.
Contriving projects with a brewer's dark.
Thus all employ themselves, and, without pity,

Leave Temple singly to be beat i' the city.

Britannia And Raleigh
Britannia.
Ah! Raleigh, when thou didst thy breath resign
To trembling James, would I had quitted mine!
Cubs didst thou call them! Hadst thou seen this brood
Of earls, and dukes, and princes of the blood,
No more of Scotish race thou wouldst complain,
These would be blessings in this spurious reign.
Awake, arise from thy long blest repose,
Once more with me partake of mortal woes!

Raleigh.
What mighty pow'r has forc'd me from my rest?
Oh! mighty Queen, why so untimely drest?

Britannia.
Favour'd by night, conceal'd in this disguise,
Whilst the lewd Court in drunken slmnbez lies,
I stole away, and never will return,
Till England knows who did her city burn;
Till Cavaliers shall favourites be deem'd
And loyal Sufferers by the Court esteem'd;
Till Leigh and Galloway shall bribes reject;
Thus O[sbor]ne's golden cheat I shall detect:
Till atheist Lauderdale shall leave this Land,
And Commons' votes shall cut-nose guards disband:
Till Kate a happy mother shall become,
Till Charles loves parliaments, and James hates Rome.

Raleigh.
What fatal crimes make you for ever fly
Your once lov'd Court, and martyr's progeny?

Britannia.
A colony of French possess the Court;
Pimps, priests, buffoons, in privy-chamber sport.
Such slimy monsters ne'er approach a throne,
Since Pharaoh's days, nor so defil'd a crown.
In sacred ear tyrannick arts they croak,
Pervert his mind, and good intentions choake,
Tell him of golden Lidies, fairy lands,
Leviathan, and absolute commands.
Thus fairy-like, the king they steal away,
And in his room a changling Lewis lay.
How oft have I him to himself restored,
In's left the scale, in 's right hand plac'd the sword?
Taught him their use, what dangers would ensue

To them who strive to separate these two?
The bloody Scotish Chronicle read o're,
Shewed him how many kings, in purple gore,
Were hurl'd to hell, by cruel tyrant lore?
The other day fam'd Spencer I did bring,
In lofty notes Tudor's blest race to sing;
How Spain's proud powers her virgin arms control'd,
Aud gold'n days in peaceful order roul'd;
How like ripe fruit she dropt from off her throne,
Full of grey hairs, good deeds, and great renown.
As the Jessean hero did appease
Saul's stormy rage, and stopt his black disease.
So the learn'd bard, with artful song, supprest
The swelling passion of his canker'd breast,
And in his heart kind influences shed
Of country love, by Truth and Justice bred.
Then to perform the cure so full begun.
To him I shew'd this glorious setting sun;
How, by her people's looks pursu'd from far,
She mounted on a bright celestial car.
Outshining Yirgo, or the Julian star.
Whilst in Truth's mirror this good scene he spy'd.
Entered a dame, bedeck'd with spotted pride,
Fair flower-de-luce within an azure field.
Her left hand bears the anolent Gallick shield,
By her usurp'd; her right a bloody sword,
Inscribed Leviathan, our soyeraign Lord;
Her tow'ry front a fiery meteor bears,
An exhalation bred of blood and tears;
Around her Jove's lewd ravnous curs complain,
Pale Death, Lust, Tortures, fill her pompous train;
She from the easy king Truth's mirrour took,
And on the ground in spitefril fall it broke;
Then frowning thus, with proud disdain she spoke:
"Are thred-bare virtues ornaments for kings?
Such poor pedantick toys teach underlings.
Do monarchs rise by virtue, or by sword?
Who e'er grew great by keeping of his word?
Virtue's a faint green-sickness to brave souls.
Dastards their hearts, their active heat controuls.
The rival gods, monarchs of th' other world,
This mortal poyson among princes hurl'd,
Fearing the mighty projects of the great
Should drive them from their proud celestial seat,
If not o'eraw'd by this new holy cheat.
Those pious frauds, too slight t'ensnare the brave,
Are proper arts the long-ear'd rout t'inslave.
Bribe hungry priests to deify your might,
To teach, your will's your only rule to rights
And sound damnation to all dare deny't.
Thus heaven's designs 'gainst heaven you shall turn.

And make them fear those powers they once did scorn.
When all the gobling interest of mankind,
By hirelings sold to you, shall be resign'd,
And by impostures, God and man betray'd,
The Church and State you safely may invade;
So boundless Lewis in full glory shines,
Whilst your starved power in legal fetters pines.
Shake off those baby-bands from your strong arms,
Henceforth be deaf to that old witch's charms;
Taste the delicious sweets of sovereign power,
'Tis royal game whole kingdoms to deflower.
Three spotless virgins to your bed I'll bring,
A sacrifice to you, their God and king.
As these grow stale, we'll harass human kind,
Hack Nature, till new pleasures you shall find,
Strong as your reign, and beauteous as your mind."
When she had spoke, a confus'd murmur rose,
Of French, Scotch, Irish, all my mortal foes;
Some English too, shame! disguis'd I spy'd.
Led all by the wise son-in-law of Hide.
With fury drunk, like bachanals, they roar,
Down with that common Magna Charta whore!
With joynt consent on helpless me they flew,
And from my Charles to a base goal me drew;
My reverend age expos'd to scorn and shame.
To prigs, bawds, whores, was made the publick game.
Frequent addresses to my Charles I send,
And my sad State did to his care commend;
But his fedr soul, transform'd by that French dame,
Had lost all sense of honour, justice, fame.
Like a tame Spinster in's Seraigl he sits,
Besieg'd by whores, buffoons, and bastards chits;
Lulled in security, rowling in Inst,
Resigns his crown to angel Carwell's trust;
Her creature O[sbor]ne the revenue steals;
False F[inc]h, knave Ang[le]sey misguide the seals.
Mac-James the Irish bigots does adore,
His French and Teague command on sea and shore.
The Scotch-scalado of our Court two isles,
False Lauderdale, with ordure, all defiles.
Thus the State's nightmarr'd by this hellish rout.
And no one left these furies to cast out.
Ah! Vindex, come, and purge the poyson'd State;
Descend, descend, e're the cure's desperate.

Raleigh.
Once more, great queen, thy darling strive to save.
Snatch him again from scandal and the grave;
Present to's thoughts his long-scorn'd parliament,
The basis of his throne and government.
In his deaf ears sound his dead father's name:

Perhaps that spell may 's erring soul reclaim:
Who knows what good effects from thence may spring!
'Tis godlike good to save a failing king.

Britannia.
Rawleigh, no more! for long in vain I've try'd
The Stewart from the tyrant to divide;
As easily learn'd virtuosos may
With the dog's blood his gentle kind convey
Into the wolf, and make him guardian turn
To th' bleating flock, by him so lately torn:
If this imperial juice once taint his blood,
'Tis by no potent antidote withstood.
Tyrants, like lep'rous kings, for public weal
Should be immur'd, lest the contagion steal
Over the whole. Th' elect of the Jessean line
To this firm law their sceptre did resign;
And shall this base tyrannick brood invade
Eternal laws, by God for mankind made?
To the serene Venetian State I'll go,
From her sage mouth fam'd principles to know;
With her the prudence of the ancients read,
To teach my people in their steps to tread;
By their great pattern such a State I'll frame,
Shall eternise a glorious lasting name.
Till then, my Raleigh, teach our noble youth
To love sobriety, and holy truth;
Watch and preside over their tender age.
Lest Court-corruption should their souls engage;
Teach them how arts, and arms, in thy young days,
Employed our youth, — not taverns, stews, and plays;
Tell them the generous scorn their race does owe
To flattery, pimping, and a gawdy show;
Teach them to scorn the Carwells, Portsmouths, Nells,
The Clevelands, O[sbor]ns, Berties, Lauderdales:
Poppaea, Tigelline, and Arteria's name,
All yield to these in lewdness, lust, and fame.
Make 'em admire the Talbots, Sydneys, Veres,
Drake, Cavendish, Blake; men void of slavish fears.
True sons of glory, pillars of the State,
On whose fam'd deeds all tongues and writers wait.
When with fierce ardour their bright souls do born.
Back to my dearest country I'll return.
Tarquin's just judge, and Caesar's equal peers,
With them I'll bring to dry my people's tears;
Publicola with healing hands shall pour
Balm in their wounds, and shall their life restore;
Greek arts, and Roman arms, in her conjoyn'd,
Shall England raise, relieve opprest mankind.
As Jove's great son th' infested globe did free
From noxious monsters, hell-born tyranny,

So shall my England, in a holy war.
In triumph lead chain'd tyrants from afar;
Her true Crusado shall at last pull down
The Turkish crescent, and the Persian sun.
Freed by thy labours, fortunate, blest Isle,
The earth shall rest, the heav'n shall on thee smile;

Tom May's Death

As one put drunk into the Packet-boat,
Tom May was hurry'd hence and did not know't.
But was amaz'd on the Elysian side,
And with an Eye uncertain, gazing wide,
Could not determine in what place he was,
For whence in Stevens ally Trees or Grass.
Nor where the Popes head, nor the Mitre lay,
Signs by which still he found and lost his way.
At last while doubtfully he all compares,
He saw near hand, as he imagin'd Ares.
Such did he seem for corpulence and port,
But 'twas a man much of another sort;
'Twas Ben that in the dusky Laurel shade
Amongst the Chorus of old Poets laid,
Sounding of ancient Heroes, such as were
The Subjects Safety, and the Rebel's Fear.
But how a double headed Vulture Eats,
Brutus and Cassius the Peoples cheats.
But seeing May he varied streight his song,
Gently to signifie that he was wrong.
Cups more then civil of Emilthian wine,
I sing (said he) and the Pharsalian Sign,
Where the Historian of the Common-wealth
In his own Bowels sheath'd the conquering health.
By this May to himself and them was come,
He found he was tranflated, and by whom.
Yet then with foot as stumbling as his tongue
Prest for his place among the Learned throng.
But Ben, who knew not neither foe nor friend,
Sworn Enemy to all that do pretend,
Rose more then ever he was seen severe,
Shook his gray locks, and his own Bayes did tear
At this intrusion. Then with Laurel wand,
The awful Sign of his supream command.
At whose dread Whisk Virgil himself does quake,
And Horace patiently its stroke does take,
As he crowds in he whipt him ore the pate
Like Pembroke at the Masque, and then did rate.
Far from these blessed shades tread back agen
Most servil' wit, and Mercenary Pen.
Polydore, Lucan, Allan, Vandale, Goth,

Malignant Poet and Historian both.
Go seek the novice Statesmen, and obtrude
On them some Romane cast similitude,
Tell them of Liberty, the Stories fine,
Until you all grow Consuls in your wine.
Or thou Dictator of the glass bestow
On him the Cato, this the Cicero.
Transferring old Rome hither in your talk,
As Bethlem's House did to Loretto walk.
Foul Architect that hadst not Eye to see
How ill the measures of these States agree.
And who by Romes example England lay,
Those but to Lucan do continue May.
But the nor Ignorance nor seeming good
Misled, but malice fixt and understood.
Because some one than thee more worthy weares
The sacred Laurel, hence are all these teares?
Must therefore all the World be set on flame,
Because a Gazet writer mist his aim?
And for a Tankard-bearing Muse must we
As for the Basket Guelphs and Gibellines be?
When the Sword glitters ore the Judges head,
And fear has Coward Churchmen silenced,
Then is the Poets time, 'tis then he drawes,
And single fights forsaken Vertues cause.
He, when the wheel of Empire, whirleth back,
And though the World disjointed Axel crack,
Sings still of ancient Rights and better Times,
Seeks wretched good, arraigns successful Crimes.
But thou base man first prostituted hast
Our spotless knowledge and the studies chast.
Apostatizing from our Arts and us,
To turn the Chronicler to Spartacus.
Yet wast thou taken hence with equal fate,
Before thou couldst great Charles his death relate.
But what will deeper wound thy little mind,
Hast left surviving Davenant still behind
Who laughs to see in this thy death renew'd,
Right Romane poverty and gratitude.
Poor Poet thou, and grateful Senate they,
Who thy last Reckoning did so largely pay.
And with the publick gravity would come,
When thou hadst drunk thy last to lead thee home.
If that can be thy home where Spencer lyes
And reverend Chaucer, but their dust does rise
Against thee, and expels thee from their side,
As th' Eagles Plumes from other birds divide.
Nor here thy shade must dwell, Return, Return,
Where Sulphrey Phlegeton does ever burn.
The Cerberus with all his Jawes shall gnash,
Megera thee with all her Serpents lash.

Thou rivited unto Ixion's wheel
Shalt break, and the perpetual Vulture feel.
'Tis just what Torments Poets ere did feign,
Thou first Historically shouldst sustain.
Thus by irrevocable Sentence cast,
May only Master of these Revels past.
And streight he vanisht in a Cloud of Pitch,
Such as unto the Sabboth bears the Witch.

Made in the USA
Columbia, SC
25 August 2024